The Leadership MILE™

The Leadership MILE™:
Motivate. Inspire. Learn. Empower.

Rudy R. Racine

ISBN 979-8-9951350-0-5

Library of Congress Control Number: 2026905918

Published by HireLearners Publishing
An imprint of HireLearners, LLC
www.HireLearners.com

First Edition 2026
Printed in the United States of America

DEDICATION

Humble beginnings...

To my wife Danielle, my son Ryan, and our baby on the way, I do this work for you and am grateful for you every day. I love you!

To the family that set the foundation and helped raise me into the man I am today, this book is for you all.

INTRODUCTION

Somewhere right now, a talented leader is losing a great employee — and has no idea why.

Not because they don't care. Not because they're lazy or incompetent. But because no one ever taught them how to lead people. They were promoted for being excellent at their job, handed a team, and expected to figure out the rest on their own.

Maybe that story sounds familiar.

Leadership is one of the few professions where people are routinely placed in charge of others before they've been given the tools to succeed. We inherit teams, navigate personalities, manage conflict, and drive performance — often while still learning what leadership actually requires. The gap between doing the work and leading others through it is wider than most people expect. And the cost of that gap shows up everywhere: in disengaged teams, in talented people who leave, in expectations that were never made clear, and in relationships that quietly erode before anyone addresses what went wrong.

This book was written for that gap.

The Leadership MILE™ — Motivate. Inspire. Learn. Empower. — is a practical, human-centered framework built for leaders at every level. Whether you're stepping into your first leadership role or refining an approach you've carried for years, the principles in these pages will give you language, structure, and direction to lead more intentionally.

I named this book *The Leadership MILE* because the word carries a double meaning. "MILE" represents the four pillars of effective leadership — but it also mirrors the distance we travel in professional growth. A mile can feel long when we're just starting out, uncertain of our footing and unsure of our voice. Yet with each step forward, we gain clarity, confidence, and momentum. Progress is rarely linear. The road is full of peaks and valleys, successes and setbacks, lessons learned and lessons relearned. My hope is that what's shared in these pages will shorten your learning curve and clear the path to greater leadership effectiveness.

I'll be honest with you throughout this book — including about my own early failures. You'll read about the first performance review where I discovered my feedback hadn't landed as feedback at all. About the team member I lost because I prioritized being liked over being clear. About the moment I realized I had been quietly silencing the people around me without ever raising my voice.

Those experiences weren't pleasant to live through. But they shaped everything in this framework.

The lessons here aren't theoretical. They come from the floor, the boardroom, the coaching sessions, and the hard conversations that don't have easy endings. I've had the opportunity to see leadership from multiple vantage points — coaching executive leaders, working alongside them, and serving in leadership roles myself. What became clear through all of it is this: leaders rarely fail because they lack intelligence or effort. They struggle because they haven't been taught how to lead people.

This book was written to help you fix that.

What We'll Cover

The goal of the Leadership MILE is to equip you with a practical, human-centered leadership approach—one that helps you build stronger relationships, create clarity, foster accountability, and drive consistent results. In this book, you'll learn how to:

- Motivate and inspire a diverse team using strategies that connect with different personalities and passions

- Communicate the "why" behind your directives in a way that builds trust and engagement

- Lead with emotional intelligence, even in moments of conflict or uncertainty

- Partner with your team to achieve meaningful, sustainable outcomes

- Measure your effectiveness as a leader through indicators like trust, engagement, retention, growth, and performance outcomes

These principles form the foundation of The Leadership MILE, guiding you through the practices that make leadership meaningful, intentional, and deeply impactful.

Measuring Your Success

Leadership effectiveness is often described as subjective—and in many ways, it is. There is no single scorecard that perfectly captures what it means to lead well. Yet despite that subjectivity, effective leadership leaves clear signals. Your team will show you—through their behavior, their results, and their willingness to follow—how your leadership approach is landing.

As you move through the Leadership MILE, you will be introduced to additional ways to assess your effectiveness within each of the four leadership pillars—Motivate, Inspire, Learn, and Empower. Each pillar offers its own indicators, helping you evaluate not just what you are achieving, but how you are leading while achieving it. These reflections are meant to sharpen your awareness and help you identify where your approach is working well and where it may need adjustment.

This book is not meant to be read once and set aside. Some ideas may resonate immediately, while others may take on new meaning as your role, your team, or your challenges evolve. I encourage you to make notes, revisit sections, and experiment with different approaches as you read. Leadership growth rarely happens all at once—it develops through reflection, application, and a willingness to learn from experience.

With that foundation in mind, we begin by stepping back and gaining clarity. Before focusing on specific skills or behaviors, it's important to clarify what leadership means to you and the kind of impact you want to have. The first chapter introduces the Leadership MILE framework and invites you to reflect on the type of leader you are becoming—setting the stage for everything that follows.

DEFINING YOUR LEADERSHIP SUCCESS

Before I introduce the Leadership MILE framework, I want to start with a story from the beginning of my leadership career. It comes from my very first formal leadership role—and it remains the most important leadership lesson I've learned. Not because I handled it perfectly, but because it forced me to confront what leadership actually requires.

I still remember stepping into the position and realizing how quickly the role changed my perspective. For the first time, I wasn't just responsible for my own performance—I was responsible for the performance, development, and experience of others. I knew how to do the work, and I did it well. What I didn't yet understand was that leading people would require a very different approach than doing the job myself.

That first year in leadership was full of lessons, but two stood out immediately. Not everyone wants to be led the way I liked to be led. And what feels like common sense to one person isn't always clear to another.

The leadership style that worked for me—independence, trust, and minimal oversight—was motivating when I was an individual contributor. But when I applied that same approach to my team, it didn't land the way I expected. What felt like empowerment to me felt like distance to some of my direct reports. Expectations that were clear in my mind weren't always clear to them. I knew what strong performance looked like, yet some team members believed they were doing excellent work when they were only meeting part of the mark.

That disconnect became impossible to ignore during my first formal performance evaluation with one of my team members.

In her self-assessment, she rated herself a 5 out of 5 across every core competency. My assessment was very different. I saw her performance as average overall, with several areas that needed improvement. What stood out most wasn't the difference in our ratings—it was what that difference revealed.

Throughout the year, I believed I had been giving feedback. In my mind, I was addressing concerns through regular conversations and informal check-ins. In her mind, we were simply having casual, friendly discussions. Because I hadn't clearly framed those conversations as feedback— or set explicit expectations around performance— she never received them as guidance meant to help her improve.

That evaluation was a wake-up call.

I realized that in trying to be approachable and supportive, I had kept things too informal. I had prioritized being liked over being clear. I was more of a buddy than the leader she needed me to be at that stage. The independence I valued wasn't what she needed. She needed structure, clarity, and consistent feedback—especially early on.

By the time I fully understood what she needed from me, the relationship had already suffered. I hadn't created the conditions that would have set her up for success, and eventually, she chose to resign. That outcome stayed with me—not because of the resignation itself, but because of what it revealed about my leadership.

This experience became my first—and greatest—leadership lesson. Effective leadership isn't about leading people the way *you* want to be led. It's about understanding who your people are, assessing what they need from you, and being intentional about how you show up as their leader.

I'm sharing this story because before we talk about frameworks, skills, or strategies, leadership begins with self-awareness. Before you can lead others well, you need clarity on the kind of leader you want to be—and the kind of leader your team needs you to become.

Your First Steps

What kind of leader do you want to be—and what kind of impact do you want your leadership to have on the people who experience it every day?

That question sits at the center of effective leadership, even though it's rarely asked directly. Leadership often begins quickly—a promotion, a new responsibility, a team placed in your care—and before there's time to reflect, people are already looking to you for direction, clarity, and support.

Rather than starting with techniques or strategies, your first step is to pause and reflect. Not just on what you need to accomplish, but on how you want to show up for the people you lead. The way your leadership is experienced—day in and day out—will shape trust, performance, and engagement far more than any single decision you make.

At the same time, effective leadership requires flexibility. While it's important to have a clear sense of the kind of leader you aspire to be, it's equally important to recognize that your team may need you to stretch beyond that definition at times. Ideally, who you want to be as a leader and what your team needs from you are closely aligned. But there will be moments when they are not—and leadership growth often happens in that gap.

Strong leaders are willing to adjust, learn, and expand their approach in service of their team. That means paying attention to how different individuals respond to your leadership, being open to feedback, and intentionally developing skills that may not come naturally. This willingness to learn and adapt will become especially important as you encounter new challenges, diverse personalities, and evolving expectations. We'll return to this idea more deeply in the Learn section of the book, but it's worth acknowledging here: leadership isn't static, and neither is the leader.

Before thinking about *how* to lead, it can be helpful to think about *the roles leaders often play*. These roles are not titles, and they are not fixed styles. They are lenses through which leadership is experienced—and most effective leaders move between them depending on what their team needs in a given moment.

The roles below are not meant to be a complete list. There are many ways leadership shows up. These examples are offered to spark reflection— to help you consider how you show up as a leader today, and to think about leaders you've worked with or for who had a lasting impact on you.

As you read through them, notice which ones resonate most, which feel less natural, and which your team may need more of right now.

Common Leadership Roles You May Recognize

The Teacher

Helps others understand what success looks like and how to achieve it. Teachers are patient, knowledgeable, and committed to helping people build the skills and confidence needed to perform well in their role.

The Listener

Creates a safe space for people to think out loud, share challenges, and explore ideas without fear of judgment. Listeners set ego aside and offer presence, understanding, and validation.

The Catalyst

Expands thinking and sparks momentum. Catalysts use stories, insights, and well-timed questions to help others see new possibilities and connect ideas in ways that move action forward.

The Accountability Partner

Holds people responsible for meeting expectations and following through on commitments. Accountability Partners don't let things slide and help others stay aligned with what they said they would do.

The Challenger

Pushes people beyond comfort and perceived limits. Challengers see potential others may not yet recognize and encourage growth that moves past mediocrity.

The Champion

Supports and celebrates others both publicly and privately. Champions advocate for people even when they aren't in the room and help build confidence through encouragement and recognition.

The Advisor
Shares wisdom gained through experience.
Advisors offer perspective, lessons learned, and
guidance that help others grow with intention.

Most leaders naturally gravitate toward some of
these roles more than others. What matters isn't
playing every role equally—it's being aware of the
roles you tend to play, the ones you avoid, and
the ones your team may need most in a given
moment.

As you reflect, consider which of these roles feel
most like you, which ones have had the greatest
impact on you when others played them, and
where you may need to stretch to better support
your team.

With that clarity in mind, the next section of the
book begins with Motivation. We'll explore what
motivation really is, why it differs from person to
person, and how effective leaders create
environments where people want to give their
best. You'll also be introduced to the five
Methods of Motivation, which will help you
better understand what drives behavior—and
how to lead in ways that truly connect.

MOTIVATE

"The best leaders don't know just one style of leadership - they're skilled at several, and have the flexibility to switch between styles as the circumstance dictates." — Daniel Goleman

The previous chapter focused on defining the kind of leader you want to be and the impact you hope your leadership will have on others. The next step is understanding how that intent shows up in practice—particularly in how you motivate the people you lead. Motivation is often where leadership becomes most visible, because it shapes how your actions are experienced day to day. By definition, motivation is the process of creating conditions that encourage people to bring effort, focus, and commitment to their work.

My understanding of motivation—and its impact on people—began early in my leadership development. I was learning in real time that the people on your team are different, and that effective leadership requires more than a single, uniform approach.

I vividly remember a period where I was tasked with leading a newly formed team and had to quickly learn who I was leading and how they responded to different leadership approaches. I hadn't had the opportunity to shape the team from the start, which meant I needed to invest time in understanding the people in front of me—how they worked, how they communicated, and what energized them.

From the beginning, I was intentional about getting to know the people behind the roles. I spent time on the floor each morning, greeting team members by name and paying attention to how they responded. Some visibly lit up during those brief interactions. Others acknowledged the greeting politely but without much energy. Even in those small moments, the team was giving me information.

As time went on, similar patterns appeared in other settings. During team meetings, some people were clearly energized by public recognition, while others seemed uncomfortable with the attention. When incentives were introduced, certain staff noticeably increased their effort, while others remained steady and unaffected. I didn't need formal assessments to see what was happening—my team was showing me, through their reactions, what worked for them and what didn't.

It was in those moments that I became aware of a lesson that would continue to show up throughout my leadership career: my team was constantly giving me clues about how they wanted to be motivated, and my responsibility as a leader was to notice those clues.

It was through that combination of observation and reflection that I developed what I now call the Five Motivational Methods: Contact, Acknowledgment, Rewards, Assistance, and Time. This framework wasn't created to label people or reduce motivation to a formula. It was created to help leaders pay closer attention, ask better questions, and lead with greater intention. I've intentionally ordered these methods to form the acronym CARAT, as a simple way to help leaders remember the full range of motivational approaches available to them.

What follows is an exploration of these five methods—not as a checklist, but as a way to expand how you understand and respond to the people you lead.

The Five Motivational Methods

Contact

Contact uses simple, appropriate physical gestures—like a handshake, high-five, or fist bump—to acknowledge effort and create connection. These gestures don't replace words or feedback. Instead, they reinforce them when used intentionally and with awareness of boundaries. When applied thoughtfully, Contact helps humanize leadership and reminds people that their effort is seen in the moment.

Contact works best during moments of progress. Celebrating a win, recognizing effort after a challenging stretch, or reinforcing a shared success are times when brief, appropriate gestures can lift morale and strengthen team chemistry. For some people, these moments create a strong sense of connection.

Human connection plays a powerful role in how people experience leadership. Small, positive interpersonal cues—eye contact, proximity, brief physical acknowledgment—can strengthen trust and reinforce a sense of belonging at work. When people feel socially connected, they are more likely to stay engaged, collaborate openly, and push through challenges rather than withdraw.

At the same time, physical gestures are never neutral. Context matters. Power dynamics matter. Culture and personal history matter. What feels encouraging to one person may feel intrusive or uncomfortable to another. That's why Contact works best when leaders remain observant and responsive rather than relying on habit or routine.

The challenge with Contact is that it carries more risk than many leaders realize. Comfort levels vary widely based on personal boundaries, culture, gender dynamics, and past experiences. Leaders have limited control over how people perceive their actions, but they have significantly more control over the optics—what they consistently model and allow to be seen by the team.

I once observed a leader who developed a playful, recurring handshake with one direct report. While the gesture itself was harmless and well-intentioned, it became a focal point for speculation among other team members. What began as a simple form of connection turned into rumors and distractions—not because of intent, but because of optics.

Contact is effective when it creates connection without confusion. You can measure its success by watching how people respond over time. Do they naturally reciprocate, or do they pull back? Does energy increase, or does discomfort surface? When Contact is motivating, it builds trust. When it becomes a distraction, it's a signal to adjust.

Acknowledgment

Acknowledgment motivates through written or verbal recognition that clearly names effort, contribution, or results. It communicates that work is seen and that it matters. When done well, Acknowledgment reinforces the behaviors you want to see more of and helps people connect their efforts to meaningful outcomes.

In professional settings, Acknowledgment may show up publicly in meetings, privately in one-on-one conversations, or through thoughtful written feedback. The most effective Acknowledgment is intentional and specific—it highlights what someone did, when it happened, why it mattered, and the impact it had. Recognition carries the most weight when it helps people understand what "good" looks like, not just that something was appreciated.

Effective acknowledgment sounds less like general praise and more like clear observation. For example:

"Yesterday, I noticed how intentionally you supported a client as they worked through our customer portal. You stayed patient, answered their questions, and made sure they felt comfortable moving forward. The client left feeling relieved and satisfied, and experiences like that make people far more likely to recommend our services. I appreciate the care you showed."

When possible, naming the specific client or situation makes acknowledgment even more meaningful. It signals that you were paying close attention and helps the recognition feel personal rather than generic.

There is also a quieter risk when acknowledgment is poorly executed. When recognition feels performative, inconsistent, or disconnected from actual contribution, trust begins to erode. Employees start questioning sincerity and fairness, and acknowledgment can shift from motivating to distracting.

I've seen this happen when recognition is treated as a routine rather than a reflection. I once managed a leader who made it a point to acknowledge someone at the start of every meeting. While the intention was good, the lack of preparation made the recognition vague and unspecific. Over time, it landed poorly—not just with the people being recognized, but with the team witnessing it.

You'll know Acknowledgment is working when confidence increases, engagement rises, and expectations become clearer across the team. You may also notice people intentionally repeating the behaviors that are being recognized—either the individual who received the acknowledgment or their peers who observed it—because they now understand what good performance looks like and how it's valued. When acknowledgment is landing well, it doesn't just feel good in the moment; it quietly shapes behavior. When it isn't working, discomfort, disengagement, or quiet resentment may surface. A helpful self-check is whether recognition feels meaningful not just to you, but to the people experiencing and observing it.

Rewards

Rewards motivate through tangible incentives tied to clearly defined outcomes. When used intentionally, they can create focus, urgency, and momentum—particularly during demanding periods or when short-term goals need attention.

In the workplace, Rewards might include bonuses, gift cards, extra time off, or other incentives tied to measurable results. For some individuals, especially those motivated by competition or tangible benchmarks, Rewards can be energizing in the short term and help sharpen focus around priority goals.

One of the most common pitfalls with Rewards isn't the incentive itself—it's the design behind it. Leaders often focus heavily on outcomes without fully accounting for the time and discipline required to administer an incentive program well. Reviewing performance, tracking progress, and determining whether criteria were met takes effort. When targets are set too high, people disengage because the reward feels unattainable. When the bar is too low, performance plateaus. And when criteria are subjective or loosely defined, frustration replaces motivation.

Another limitation of Rewards is that they tend to lose power over time when they become the primary driver of behavior. When incentives dominate, people may begin optimizing for the reward rather than the quality or purpose of the work itself. Once the reward disappears, so does the motivation.

I remember noticing a pattern while supporting one of my leaders who leaned heavily on Rewards as her primary way of motivating her team. Her belief was simple and well-intentioned: if people were financially incentivized, performance would follow. At first, it did. But as time went on, a subtle shift occurred. Some team members started confusing effort with results. They worked hard, stayed busy, and felt frustrated when rewards didn't come—even when outcomes fell short. What became clear was that the incentive had started to matter more than the impact of the work itself.

Rewards are most effective when they reinforce purpose rather than replace it. Leaders should look beyond immediate gains and pay attention to what remains once incentives are removed. When designed thoughtfully and applied consistently, Rewards can energize performance. Sustainable motivation shows up when people continue to perform even when rewards are not on the table.

Assistance

Assistance motivates through support. It shows up when leaders step in to remove barriers, help during high-pressure moments, or work alongside their team to get the job done. For many employees, Assistance signals care, solidarity, and commitment from leadership. It communicates that leadership is present and willing to share the weight of the work—sometimes by rolling up their sleeves when it truly matters.

Support is especially important during periods of uncertainty or transition. When leaders are willing to assist at the right moments, people are more likely to stay engaged and push through challenges. It reinforces the belief that leadership understands the work, the pressure, and the realities on the ground.

While Assistance offers real benefits, it also requires a healthy dose of restraint. When overused, it can unintentionally limit growth—especially when a leader steps in to remove every challenge before team members can work through them. Growth often accelerates when team members are supported without being shielded from every obstacle. When people are encouraged to think, adapt, and respond—while knowing leadership is available if needed—learning deepens. Occasional missteps, paired with reflection and guidance, tend to strengthen confidence far more than uninterrupted success.

Early in my leadership career, I learned this lesson firsthand. I remember leaning heavily on Assistance, not only because I enjoyed doing the work, but because I felt a responsibility to demonstrate credibility. Working alongside my team helped build trust and showed that I understood the job they were being asked to do. Over time, I realized I wasn't giving my team the space they needed to grow. They needed room to make decisions, test ideas, and even make mistakes. My role wasn't to prevent every misstep —it was to stay connected enough that those missteps became lessons, not liabilities. When I gave people space to propose solutions and checked in to guide their thinking, growth accelerated and accountability became clearer.

Assistance works best when it is used intentionally. When leaders step in strategically, they remind their team that they are not alone— that support is available and leadership is invested in their success. Occasional involvement reinforces connection and confidence, while stepping back at the right moments preserves ownership. That balance helps people feel supported without being rescued and accountable without feeling abandoned.

If everything consistently flows through you, it may be time to step back. If your presence builds confidence while preserving ownership, Assistance is doing exactly what it's meant to do.

Time

Time motivates through presence and focused attention. When leaders give their time well, it communicates value without needing words. Consistent one-on-ones, meaningful check-ins, and intentional conversations help people feel heard, supported, and aligned. For many employees, time is the clearest signal that their leader genuinely cares.

I once worked for a leader who used time exceptionally well. When we met, distractions were removed, prior conversations were remembered, and space was intentionally created for me to talk about my team, my priorities, and where I needed support. That presence made me more prepared, more engaged, and more invested in my work. I grew significantly under that leadership—not because meetings were long, but because the time we spent together actually mattered.

One of the most common challenges leaders raise is simply this: "I don't have time to meet with everyone regularly." Research consistently shows, however, that regular one-on-one meetings are one of the most effective tools leaders have. Studies on manager effectiveness and employee engagement indicate that employees who meet with their manager at least bi-weekly report higher engagement, clearer expectations, and stronger trust. Some research even points to weekly check-ins as ideal—particularly in fast-moving or people-intensive environments—but consistency matters more than duration.

For leaders who feel overwhelmed or believe they can't afford an hour-long meeting, the answer isn't to avoid meeting altogether—it's to start smaller and be intentional. A focused 15-minute check-in, when done well, can be far more motivating than a distracted hour. What matters most is presence, clarity, and follow-through. Even brief, consistent touch-points send a powerful message: you matter, and your work matters.

When Time is used poorly, the contrast is unmistakable. Meetings can feel wasteful or performative when leaders are distracted by emails or phone calls, book time without a clear purpose, or dominate the conversation with their own priorities. Time can also feel intrusive when leaders schedule excessive check-ins, request constant updates, or insist on reviewing every detail before work can move forward. In both cases—whether through distraction or over-involvement—Time stops feeling supportive and starts getting in the way of real work.

Used intentionally, Time creates alignment, trust, and momentum. Used carelessly, it creates frustration, disengagement, and fatigue. The difference isn't how much time you spend; it's how intentionally you show up.

Time is working when conversations feel focused, reciprocal, and productive—when issues surface earlier and expectations are clear. It stops working when meetings feel distracted, excessive, or unnecessary. Few things motivate people more than feeling genuinely supported—and few things demotivate faster than realizing their time is not being respected.

Expanding Your Range as a Leader

Understanding the Five Motivational Methods is only the starting point. The real work begins when you reflect on how each of these methods shows up through you as a leader. No two leaders demonstrate Contact, Acknowledgment, Rewards, Assistance, or Time in exactly the same way—and that's not a flaw, it's reality.

Your approach will be shaped by your personality, your experiences, your comfort level, and the environment you lead in. There is no perfect formula or fixed ratio of these methods that works for every team. What motivates one group may fall flat with another, and what works well today may need to be adjusted months from now as your team evolves, roles change, or new challenges emerge.

That's why motivation isn't something you set once and move on from. It's something you continually assess. Your responsibility as a leader is to pay attention—to notice how your team responds to your presence, your feedback, your support, and your expectations. Those responses are clues. They tell you when a particular approach is landing and when it's time to shift.

With a clear understanding of the Five Motivational Methods, you're better equipped to recognize those signals and make intentional choices about how you show up. Sometimes that means leaning in. Other times it means pulling back. Effective motivation isn't about doing more—it's about doing what fits the moment and the people in front of you.

Motivation helps people move. But movement alone isn't enough.

Measuring Success: Motivate

Measuring motivation is one of the more nuanced leadership challenges because motivation itself is internal. You cannot observe it directly — you can only observe what it produces. That makes the measurement less about formal assessments and more about deliberate attention to the signals your team is already sending you every day.

The most reliable place to start is how your team shows up. Not just physically, but energetically. Are people arriving ready to engage, or are they going through the motions? Is there a noticeable difference in someone's energy on certain days or during certain types of work? Motivation tends to be visible in small moments — the person who lingers after a meeting to share an idea, the team member who takes extra care on a task they didn't have to, the colleague who jumps in to help without being asked. These aren't dramatic signals. They are quiet ones. But they are consistent, and over time they paint a clear picture.

Effort is another important indicator — and it's worth distinguishing between effort and activity. A motivated employee doesn't just stay busy. They invest. They bring care to their work, ask questions that go beyond what's required, and push for quality even when no one is checking. When you notice that someone is doing the minimum — technically meeting expectations but nothing more — that gap between capability and contribution is often a motivational signal worth exploring.

Engagement in team settings provides a third layer of measurement. Pay attention to who contributes during meetings and who has gone quiet. Notice whether participation feels voluntary or obligated. A team that is motivated tends to generate discussion, challenge ideas constructively, and leave meetings with energy rather than exhaustion. When contributions dry up — when the same voices carry every conversation and others simply observe — motivation may be eroding somewhere in the room.

Discretionary effort may be the most telling measure of all. Discretionary effort is what people choose to give beyond what is expected — volunteering for a project, mentoring a newer colleague, flagging a problem before it escalates. It cannot be required, and it cannot be incentivized into existence. It shows up when people feel genuinely connected to their work, their team, and their leader. When you see it, take note. When it disappears, take that note too.

A useful self-check for leaders is to think through each member of your team individually and ask: when did I last see this person give discretionary effort? If you struggle to answer that question for someone, it may be worth reflecting on which of the CARAT methods you have been using with them recently — and whether your approach is still aligned with what motivates them most.

One important caution: changes in motivation are not always about leadership. Life circumstances, personal challenges, team dynamics, and role fit all influence how people show up. The goal of measurement is not to assign blame but to stay informed — to notice shifts early enough to respond with curiosity rather than frustration. A timely, genuine check-in is often more valuable than any formal assessment, and it is almost always the right first step when something feels off.

Motivation is not a problem to be solved once. It is a condition to be tended to consistently. The leaders who do this best are not the ones running the most sophisticated tracking systems — they are the ones paying close enough attention to notice when something has changed, and caring enough to do something about it.

In the next chapter, we'll explore Inspire—how leaders connect direction to meaning, translate goals into purpose, and help people understand why their work matters. While motivation influences behavior, inspiration shapes belief. And when leaders learn to do both well, their impact deepens.

INSPIRE

"There are only two ways to influence human behavior: you can manipulate it or you can inspire it." — Simon Sinek

One of the most common leadership mistakes is assuming that motivation and inspiration are the same thing. They are closely related, but they are not interchangeable. Motivation influences behavior—it helps people take action, apply effort, and stay engaged. Inspiration shapes meaning—it helps people understand why the work matters and why their effort is worth sustaining.

Simon Sinek's quote introduces an uncomfortable truth many leaders never pause to examine: leadership that relies solely on motivation, without inspiration, can begin to feel manipulative. When people are driven primarily by incentives, pressure, fear of consequences, or constant urgency—without a clear sense of purpose—they may comply, but they rarely commit. Over time, motivation without meaning turns work into a transaction.

Effective leaders learn to balance both. They know how to motivate when action is required, deadlines matter, or performance needs a boost. But they also know how to inspire—how to connect direction to purpose, translate goals into meaning, and help people see their work as more than a series of tasks.

In this chapter, we turn our attention to Inspire. We'll explore how leaders build belief and sustain commitment by adapting how they communicate, by using story to convey meaning, and by modeling resilience when circumstances are challenging. Inspiration doesn't always come from what you say; it often comes from how your message connects to what others care about.

Becoming a "Multilingual" Leader

One of the most powerful ways leaders inspire is by learning how to frame their message so it resonates with different people on their team. I use the term "Multilingual Leader" to describe leaders who demonstrate the flexibility to communicate purpose in ways that connect with different perspectives, priorities, and emotional drivers.

This isn't about changing expectations or lowering standards. It's about translating those expectations into language that people can hear. The same directive can land very differently depending on how it's framed. What feels logical and compelling to one person may feel disconnected or even dismissive to another.

As we discussed in the Motivation chapter, people respond to different signals. Inspiration builds on that insight. Some people connect deeply to impact. Others connect to growth, stability, the quality of the work being done, or responsibility to others. A Multilingual Leader pays attention to those differences and adjusts how they communicate purpose accordingly.

Think about leaders you've worked for who made you want to give more than what was required. Chances are, they didn't inspire you by repeating policies or metrics. They inspired you by speaking in a way that connected to something you cared about. That ability—to translate vision into language that resonates—is at the heart of inspirational leadership.

A Story of Misalignment

A few years ago, I was hired to coach a leader who was struggling to inspire his team to change. The Board had brought him in for his reputation of driving performance and his passion for the organization's mission. On paper, he was the right choice. In practice, he quickly ran into resistance.

Within months of starting the role, he found himself bumping heads with a long-tenured leader on his team—someone who had been with the organization for over a decade and was deeply respected by staff and community partners. During one of our early coaching sessions, he vented his frustration. He felt that she resisted every change he tried to introduce. He also believed she questioned his authority and may have felt she should have been in his position.

From her perspective, the story looked very different. She had lived through multiple leadership transitions and felt she was the steady presence protecting the heart of the work. She believed the team was performing well, the community was satisfied, and change felt unnecessary—especially from a leader she wasn't convinced would be there long-term.

The issue wasn't a lack of intelligence, commitment, or care. Both leaders were deeply invested. The problem was perspective.

The leader I was coaching framed his directives almost exclusively around compliance, performance metrics, and organizational expectations. The messages were logical, accurate, and well intentioned—but they didn't connect to what his team valued most. His words emphasized what needed to change, but not why it mattered to the people doing the work.

In our coaching sessions, we focused on one shift: reframing his message to connect expectations to impact. Rather than opening conversations with compliance language, he began grounding proposed changes in the real consequences for the people and programs his team cared about most. He talked about how small gaps in process could jeopardize partnerships the organization had worked years to build, how missed requirements could threaten funding for initiatives families relied on, and how protecting those resources meant protecting the very clients and community outcomes the staff took pride in delivering.

Nothing about the expectation changed. But the meaning did.

Once his message aligned with what the team was passionate about, resistance softened. Conversations became more productive. Momentum followed. He didn't inspire through authority—he inspired through connection. That shift marked the beginning of his growth into a Multilingual Leader.

The Power of Perspective

The image above represents the conflict described in the "Story of Misalignment" I just shared, and it illustrates a simple but powerful truth about leadership.

Two individuals stand on opposite sides of the same number. One sees a six. The other sees a nine. Both are confident. Both are certain. Both are technically correct—based on where they are standing.

The conflict does not stem from intelligence or intent. It stems from perspective.

In leadership, this dynamic plays out constantly. A leader may see urgency, risk, and strategic necessity. A team member may see stability, history, and what is already working. The facts may be the same. The interpretation is not.

When leaders attempt to inspire action without first acknowledging perspective, they often encounter resistance. Not because their team lacks commitment, but because the message has been delivered from only one vantage point.

The expectation of leadership is not simply to defend your position more clearly. It is to momentarily step to the other side of the number.

Imagine how quickly the argument in the image would dissolve if either person paused, walked around, and viewed the number from the other side. The debate would shift from "I'm right and you're wrong" to "I see why you're seeing what you're seeing."

That shift changes everything.

When leaders take the time to understand how their team interprets a directive—what they fear, what they value, what they believe is at risk—they gain the ability to frame their message in a way that connects. This is where perspective fuels inspiration.

Understanding your own view is important. Understanding your team's view is transformational.

This ability strengthens your growth as a Multilingual Leader. It allows you to translate vision without diluting it, to hold standards while honoring context, and to inspire action without creating division.

And once perspective is acknowledged, leaders can move beyond explanation and into something even more powerful: helping people feel the why.

Conveying the Why Through Story

Sometimes inspiration requires more than reframing directives. Sometimes it requires telling a story to light a fire inside a team member.

Stories are one of the most effective ways humans make sense of complexity. They engage emotion, create connection, and allow people to picture themselves inside the work. Data informs, but stories move. An effective story doesn't just explain what needs to change—it helps people feel why the change matters.

Research across psychology and neuroscience consistently shows that people are far more likely to remember, internalize, and act on information when it's delivered in narrative form rather than as isolated facts or instructions. Stories engage both logic and emotion, helping people connect effort to meaning instead of treating work as a series of disconnected tasks.

To make storytelling more accessible and intentional for leaders, I rely on a simple framework that can be used in everything from staff meetings to one-on-one conversations:

Capture → Obstacle → Response → Outcome → Call to Action

Capture is where you earn attention. This may be a sentence, a moment, or a short reflection that causes people to pause and lean in. It might sound like, *"I want to share something impactful I noticed last week…"* or *"There's a moment from my career that keeps coming to mind right now."* The goal isn't drama—it's curiosity.

Obstacle names the challenge. This is the tension, barrier, or reality that made action necessary. Obstacles give stories relevance. They answer the unspoken question: *Why does this matter right now?*

Response explains how the obstacle was addressed. This is where leadership shows up. You outline the decisions made, the behaviors demonstrated, or the mindset adopted in response to the challenge. This part of the story is especially powerful because it models what "good" looks like.

Outcome describes what resulted—or what you are trying to achieve. This might be a real outcome from the past or a future outcome you're inviting the team to work toward. Either way, it connects action to impact.

Call to Action brings the story back to the present. It's where you invite your team to act. This might sound like confidence in their ability to replicate the response, or a clear ask tied directly to the story you just told.

This structure works because it mirrors how people naturally process experience. We understand the world through challenge, response, and consequence. When leaders tell stories this way, they aren't embellishing reality— they're helping others see how effort connects to outcomes and how today's actions shape tomorrow's results.

Rather than searching for the perfect story, leaders are often better served by looking at the experiences they already carry. Many moments we dismiss as "just part of the job" can be deeply inspiring to others—especially to people who are earlier in their journey, facing uncertainty, or questioning whether they're capable of what's being asked of them.

As a leader, it's worth pausing to reflect on your current role and asking yourself: *Where might I already have a story that could help my team move forward?* It might be a moment when you doubted yourself and stepped forward anyway. It might be a setback that forced you to adapt. It might be a decision that felt uncomfortable at the time but proved necessary in hindsight.

To begin identifying those stories, take a few minutes to jot down brief notes using the framework:

- What moment would capture attention?

- What obstacle were you facing?

- How did you respond?

- What was the outcome, or what did you learn?

- What call to action does that story invite from your team?

You don't need to over-polish these stories. Authenticity matters far more than eloquence. Sometimes the stories we discount as ordinary are the very ones someone else needs to hear. You will never know the impact your story might have on someone until you choose to share it. Your audience is waiting.

Inspiring Through Resilience

Adapting your messaging to meet your team members where they are, acknowledging different perspectives, and using storytelling are all effective techniques to inspire action. An additional tactic that leaders can use to inspire has less to do with what you say, and more to do with how you show up.

Think back to a time when a leader helped you or your team navigate through a challenging period. Maybe a key initiative stalled. Maybe funding shifted, expectations changed, or pressure intensified overnight. What likely stayed with you wasn't just what that leader said—it was how they showed up when uncertainty entered the room.

One of the most powerful—and often overlooked—sources of inspiration is resilience.

Resilient leaders don't pretend challenges don't exist. They acknowledge reality, stay grounded, and help others move forward with clarity and confidence. They regulate their own reactions before responding publicly. They create space for solutions instead of amplifying panic. That steadiness communicates something powerful without ever needing to say it directly.

Demonstrating resilience can be done by embracing the "Event + Response = Outcome" framework—often shortened to E + R = O—popularized by best-selling author Jack Canfield. The premise is simple but profound: while we don't always control the events we face, we always control how we respond—and that response often shapes the outcome.

In practice, resilient leadership is not passive acceptance. It is active choice.

When a setback occurs, resilient leaders pause before reacting. They ask themselves not only, *"What response protects me?"* but also, *"What response best serves my team?"* They work alongside their teams to unpack what happened and guide them toward a constructive next step.

Instead of allowing an obstacle to stall
momentum, they might ask:

- What part of this situation is within our
  control?

- What response will move us closer to our
  long-term goal?

- If we look back on this moment a year
  from now, what response will we be proud
  of?

By modeling this thinking out loud, leaders coach
their teams in real time. They demonstrate that
while events may be disruptive, they do not
dictate destiny. The response does.

This is also where resilience begins to strengthen what Harvard Professor Dr. Amy Edmondson calls psychological safety—not in the abstract sense of comfort, but in the practical sense of how teams respond to difficulty. Psychological safety, at its core, is the shared belief that setbacks, mistakes, and challenges can be discussed openly without fear of blame or humiliation. When leaders respond to obstacles with composure and curiosity rather than frustration or defensiveness, they signal that the team can openly discuss problems without escalating fear. That safety allows learning to replace avoidance and momentum to replace paralysis.

When leaders consistently model this mindset and invite their teams into it, setbacks become learning moments instead of failure points. Pressure becomes manageable. Confidence grows —not because conditions are perfect, but because people trust their collective ability to respond effectively.

Resilience inspires because it communicates steadiness.
It tells people: we may not control the event, but we can control what happens next.

Measuring Success: Inspire

Measuring inspiration isn't done by focusing on enthusiasm alone. It requires you to pay attention to consistency, ownership, and resilience over time. Inspired teams don't just execute tasks—they internalize purpose. They understand how their work connects to something larger, and they remain engaged even when progress feels slow.

You'll often see inspiration reflected in how people talk about their work. Conversations shift from rules and requirements to impact and outcomes. Initiative increases. Setbacks are met with problem-solving rather than blame. Alignment replaces constant oversight.

Another powerful indicator of inspiration is retention. Employees who feel connected to a leader's vision—and who believe their work matters—are significantly less likely to leave. While turnover can be influenced by many factors, leaders can conduct a simple retention check. Look back six months and identify how many team members were working under your leadership at that time. How many of those same individuals are still on your team today? Promotions and internal transfers should not count against you—they are signs of growth. If you've been leading the team for at least a year, repeat the same reflection over a twelve-month period. Patterns in retention often reveal whether people feel inspired to stay and grow, or whether something is missing.

One of the most effective ways to assess inspiration is through reflection.

Self-Check for Leaders

- Do my team members understand why their work matters?

- Do people show ownership even when I'm not present?

- When change is introduced, does curiosity outweigh resistance?

- How do I respond when things don't go as planned?

- Am I consistently connecting expectations to meaning?

Leaders can also take this a step further by anonymously surveying their team. These same questions can be reframed as rating statements and scored on a scale of 1 to 5. For example: *"I understand how my work contributes to the organization's mission."* Tracking the percentage of employees who rate statements at a 4 or 5 can provide a measurable snapshot of inspirational impact. Keep in mind, surveys are less effective with fewer than five direct reports, as anonymity becomes harder to preserve and candor may decrease.

Ultimately, inspiration is not about charisma or speeches. It is about alignment. It is about helping people see meaning in their effort and believe their contribution matters.

Motivation helps people move.
Inspiration helps them believe.

In this chapter, we explored how leaders inspire by translating vision in ways that resonate, by honoring perspective, by using story to spark emotion, and by modeling resilience when challenges arise. But belief is only sustained when leaders continue to grow themselves.

In the next chapter—Learn—we turn inward. We'll explore how listening, feedback, and communication shape a leader's ability to continuously improve and deepen connection. Inspiration opens the door. Learning keeps it open.

LEARN

"The most basic of all human needs is the need to understand and be understood. The best way to understand people is to listen to them."
— Ralph Nichols

In the Leadership MILE framework, we've explored how leaders Motivate action and Inspire belief. Motivation helps people move. Inspiration helps them understand why movement matters. But neither pillar is sustainable without the third: Learn.

If motivation sparks effort and inspiration shapes meaning, learning ensures growth. It is the pillar that allows leaders to refine their approach, deepen connection, and continuously adapt to the people they serve. In the previous chapter, we examined how leaders connect direction to purpose and translate vision into language that resonates. This chapter turns inward. Before you can effectively inspire others, you must learn how to better understand them.

Learning is the quiet engine behind effective leadership. Every interaction with an employee—whether it's a formal meeting, a quick check-in, or an unexpected moment in the hallway—is an opportunity to learn more about them. How they communicate. How they process information. What motivates them. What drains them. What they care deeply about.

When leaders adopt this mindset, there are no losses—only lessons. Every conversation becomes a chance to improve how you deliver a message, strengthen connection, and get more out of the relationship. Even conversations that don't go well offer valuable insight, if you're willing to reflect on them.

At the center of learning is one essential skill: listening.

When I Realized I Was a "Silencer"

Before I detail how listening complements the Learn pillar, I want to share a bit about my personal listening journey. Several years ago, I took a trip out west to spend a few days with my older brother. While there, I remember noticing something uncomfortable about how I was communicating with him. During our conversations, I constantly interrupted his thoughts to insert my own. I would finish his sentences. I assumed I already knew where he was going with the points he made. Some might say I was being a typical New Yorker. From my perspective, I was being efficient, I was saving time to let him know that I understood what he was saying without the need for him to keep going.

He never called me out on it. But after a few days, I noticed he began talking less.

It was around that time that it hit me. My interruptions weren't speeding up our conversations. They were making him less interested in having them.

It was on that trip that I coined the term "Silencer" to describe the kind of listener I realized I was, and the impact I might be having on others. A "Silencer" is someone who doesn't truly listen—someone whose words, actions, or even presence unintentionally drown out the thoughts and ideas of the people around them. Silencers aren't always loud. They aren't always aggressive. In many cases, they believe they are being helpful, efficient, or decisive.

After spending that time with my brother, I remember thinking about how often I interrupted the people around me, more specifically coworkers and direct reports. I recognized how frequently I dominated conversations, usually under the assumption that I had the best or fastest solution, and how common it was for me to jump in before others could fully express their thoughts.

What I slowly began to notice was subtle—but important. In meetings, people would pause when it looked like I was going to speak. Some would shorten their explanations. Others would simply nod and let me run with my ideas. Over time, a few team members completely stopped offering ideas unless I asked directly. And eventually, I saw something else: people would simply wait for me to offer solutions to problems because if their ideas differed from mine, it might lead to a debate. It pains me to remember those days, I feel like I was unbearable.

As a leader, you are only as strong as the collective intelligence of your team, and that was an idea I didn't yet have the maturity to fully embrace. That trip to visit my brother—and the realization that followed—sparked a period of growth for me.

I began to understand something I had missed.

When you drown out ideas—even unintentionally —you miss out on better solutions. You miss creativity. You miss growth. And over time, you create an environment where people no longer feel safe sharing openly. They begin filtering their thoughts. They hesitate before speaking. They choose silence over the risk of offering an idea that doesn't align with yours.

In the previous chapter, we discussed psychological safety in the context of resilience—how teams need to feel safe discussing setbacks without fear of blame. That same concept applies here.

Psychological safety isn't only tested in moments of crisis. It's shaped in everyday conversations.

Harvard professor Dr. Amy Edmondson describes psychological safety as the shared belief that a team is safe for "interpersonal risk-taking". In other words, it means people feel comfortable speaking up, offering ideas, admitting mistakes, and asking questions without fear of embarrassment or punishment. I wasn't punishing anyone. I wasn't raising my voice. But my interruptions were quietly sending a message: your full thought isn't necessary.

When leaders interrupt, dismiss, or dominate conversations—even unintentionally—that safety weakens. When leaders slow down, listen deeply, and create space, safety strengthens—and performance follows.

That realization didn't transform me overnight. It required discipline. It required awareness. It required practice.

I began consciously slowing down. I stopped finishing people's sentences. I allowed silence to linger. I resisted the urge to solve too quickly. And over time, I saw a shift. People began contributing more freely. Conversations deepened. Ideas improved. Meetings felt collaborative rather than competitive.

Listening is not just about being polite. It's about protecting the environment where thinking happens.

And that begins with understanding what listening truly requires.

Learning Through Listening

Have you ever been in a conversation, debate, or argument where you thought you heard what someone said, responded confidently—and were met with, "You're not listening to me. That's not what I said."?

That moment is familiar, frustrating, and incredibly common in leadership.

In most cases, the breakdown isn't caused by bad intent. It's caused by divided attention. Leaders are often listening while simultaneously preparing a response, forming a counterpoint, or thinking three steps ahead. The result is partial understanding—and employees walking away feeling misunderstood.

Your ability to listen well—and respond in a way that makes people feel heard—is one of the strongest predictors of your success as a leader. The person on the other side of the conversation is the one who should experience the feeling of being heard. Many leaders assume they are strong listeners simply because they remain silent while others speak. Silence alone does not equal understanding.

To truly be considered an effective listener, the most valuable opinion belongs to the person you are communicating with. If they don't feel heard after a conversation with you, there is a strong possibility that you have room to grow in your listening.

To help you assess how you most frequently show up, the next sections will break listening into three distinct levels: Subjective, Objective, and Intuitive. In those sections, I'll describe each level and provide examples of what it might sound like to the people you're communicating with. Once you understand the differences, you'll be able to identify where you are—and what it takes to elevate your listening and improve the quality of your conversations.

Levels of Listening

Subjective Listening: Listening to Respond

Subjective listening is the most common—and lowest—level of listening. It happens when the leader is primarily focused on making their point. You hear parts of what the other person is saying, but your attention is already shifting toward how you'll respond. This is the level that most often results in the response I shared earlier: "That's not what I said."

You may reference a phrase or two from what was said, but you're not fully absorbing the message. Employees often leave these conversations feeling talked at rather than heard.

Most of us default to this level under stress, time pressure, or when emotions are involved. In fact, many leaders don't even realize they are doing it. Subjective listening is often unconscious—it's the brain's attempt to maintain efficiency and control the conversation.

If you recognize yourself here, give yourself grace. The goal is not perfection. The goal is awareness. As we discussed earlier, there are no losses—only lessons. Every time you catch yourself listening to respond instead of listening to understand, you've gained an opportunity to improve your next interaction.

Awareness is the first step toward growth.

Objective Listening: Listening to Understand

Objective listening—sometimes referred to as Active Listening—requires intentional focus. The goal isn't to respond. It's to understand.

At this level, the leader makes a deliberate effort to reflect back what they heard using phrases like:

- "What I'm hearing is…"

- "Let me make sure I understand…"

- "So what I hear you saying is…"

This approach does two important things. First, it forces you to slow down and truly pay attention. Second, it gives the employee an opportunity to clarify or correct the message if it didn't land as intended.

Objective listening also reduces costly errors. When you confirm what you heard before acting on it, you eliminate assumptions. In fast-moving environments, small misunderstandings can lead to missed deadlines, compliance issues, damaged relationships, or unnecessary rework. A simple clarification—"Let me make sure I understand this correctly..."—can prevent problems that would otherwise take hours, days, or even months to correct. Listening well is not just relational. It is operational.

Objective listening communicates: I hear you, and I care enough to get this right.

It also builds trust over time. When employees consistently hear their own thoughts accurately reflected back to them, psychological safety begins to grow. They feel safer sharing ideas, raising concerns, and speaking honestly—because they trust they won't be misrepresented.

Objective listening takes discipline. It requires you to temporarily quiet the internal voice that wants to fix, defend, or counter. When practiced consistently, conversations become calmer, clearer, and far more productive.

Intuitive Listening: Listening Beyond the Words

Think back to a conversation where you felt truly understood—where the person speaking with you captured the emotion underneath your words. They didn't just repeat what you said. They grasped what you were feeling. That is intuitive listening.

Intuitive listening goes a step beyond objective listening. It involves paying attention not only to what is being said, but how it's being said—tone, pacing, body language, and emotional cues.

This level of listening attempts to connect with the feeling beneath the message. It signals empathy. It communicates, I see you—not just your words.

Intuitive listening is powerful—but it must be handled carefully.

Labeling emotions too directly—"You sound angry" or "You seem frustrated"—can trigger defensiveness. Even when your intention is positive, the wrong wording can make someone feel minimized or judged.

I've found greater success using softer language, such as acknowledging how draining or heavy something must feel.

For example:

"Wow, thank you for sharing that. Hearing about everything you've been juggling at work and at home, I can only imagine how draining that must be."

This invites connection without defensiveness. When done well, intuitive listening helps employees feel deeply understood—even when solutions aren't immediate.

When you step back and look at these three levels, you may recognize that you move between them depending on the situation. Under pressure, you may default to subjective listening. With intention, you can operate at the objective level. And with emotional awareness and maturity, you can step into intuitive listening.

The goal is not to permanently live at the highest level. The goal is to become conscious of where you are—and choose the level that best serves the conversation in front of you.

Your listening sets the tone for everything that follows. If someone feels misunderstood, any feedback you offer will likely be filtered through defensiveness. If they feel heard, they are far more open to growth.

And that brings us to the next critical skill within the Learn pillar: delivering feedback in a way that builds growth rather than resistance.

Delivering Feedback

Listening is foundational—but learning as a leader also means knowing how to deliver feedback when performance needs correction.

For many leaders, this is the uncomfortable part of the job. Tough conversations are rarely anyone's favorite responsibility. It is much easier to celebrate wins than to address missed expectations. At the same time, having difficult conversations is not optional in leadership—it is part of the role. In many ways, it is one of the reasons leaders are compensated at a higher level than their direct reports. You are not just paid to maintain harmony. You are paid to protect standards, reinforce accountability, and develop people.

Delivering feedback is one of the most challenging parts of leadership. Done poorly, it can damage confidence, erode trust, and even push strong employees out the door. Done well, it creates clarity, growth, and alignment.

When feedback is delivered effectively, employees walk away with two important understandings. First, they are clear on what needs to improve or shift. Second, they leave the conversation knowing that they are still valued and that their contribution matters. When those two elements are present together, feedback becomes developmental rather than discouraging.

There are many feedback models available to leaders. Rather than overwhelm you with theory, I want to focus on three practical approaches that I've seen work in real-world leadership settings. Just as we explored different levels of listening, the goal here is awareness and choice. I'll walk through each approach, provide examples of what it might sound like in practice, and offer guidance on when each model may be most effective—so you can determine what best fits your team and the situation in front of you.

Situation–Behavior–Impact (SBI Approach)

The SBI approach is one of the clearest and most grounded ways to deliver feedback. It removes guesswork and keeps the conversation rooted in observable facts rather than emotion.

It follows a simple structure:

Situation – When and where did this occur?
Behavior – What specifically did the employee do?
Impact – What was the result of that behavior?

For example:

*"In this morning's strategy meeting **(Situation)**, I noticed you were on your phone for a significant portion of the discussion and didn't contribute when we were reviewing next quarter's priorities **(Behavior)**. It gave the impression that you were disengaged, and more importantly, it meant you may have missed the opportunity to share how those priorities impact your work and to confirm your understanding of what will be expected of you **(Impact)**."*

You might continue:

"If you walk out of meetings like that without full clarity, it can create unnecessary pressure later—both for you and for the team—when deadlines approach and expectations aren't aligned."

This model works because it reduces ambiguity. It focuses on what happened rather than who the person is. It keeps feedback behavioral—not personal.

When employees clearly understand the impact of their actions—especially how it affects their own success—they are more likely to adjust without feeling attacked.

However, there is one critical piece that leaders must not overlook.

If you stop at Situation–Behavior–Impact, you've raised awareness—but you haven't provided direction. The employee may understand what went wrong, but they may not be clear on what "right" looks like.

After identifying the situation, behavior, and impact, the leader must clearly articulate the desired behavior and the positive impact that change will create.

For example:

*"In future meetings, I need you to remain fully present and engaged—phone away unless it's urgent—and actively contribute your perspective, especially when we're discussing strategic direction **(Desired Behavior)**. When you do that, you protect your own clarity, reduce avoidable stress later, and position yourself as a leader in the room **(Positive Impact)**."*

Now the feedback does more than correct—it guides.

Using SBI effectively means walking the line between pointing out what needs to change and equipping the employee with a clear picture of what success looks like. When done well, it builds accountability without damaging confidence— and it turns feedback into forward movement rather than frustration.

Build–Break–Build (The Sandwich Approach)

The Sandwich Approach begins by acknowledging something the employee is doing well, followed by clear and direct constructive feedback, and closing with reinforcement that rebuilds confidence.

Using the same example from the SBI model, imagine addressing the employee who appeared disengaged during the meeting:

Build:

"I want to start by saying that you're usually one of the most engaged voices in our meetings. You consistently bring thoughtful ideas and challenge us in productive ways. That's part of what makes your presence valuable."

Break:

"Yesterday, though, I noticed you were on your phone for much of the discussion about next quarter's priorities. It gave the impression that you were disengaged, and it also meant you may have missed important context about how these changes will impact your role."

Build:

*"I value your perspective, and I want to make
sure your voice is part of these conversations.
When you're fully engaged, the team benefits
from your insight."*

Because this employee has a history of strong
engagement, this approach also creates space for
something equally important: a check-in.

You might follow up with:
*"Is everything okay? This felt a little different
than your usual presence in meetings."*

Feedback discussions are not just about
correction. They're also an opportunity to take
the temperature of your team. Sometimes
disengagement is a discipline issue. Other times,
it's a signal that something has shifted—and your
role as a leader is to be curious enough to notice.

This approach works well for employees who
need encouragement alongside accountability.

Here's where many leaders hesitate. They'll pause
and push back and ask,
*"What if the employee is a terror and I can't think
of anything positive about them to start the
feedback with?"*

My response is always the same: there is always something positive. The challenge is not the absence of good—it's a lack of awareness.

When a leader is frustrated with an employee, it's easy to focus only on what's wrong. But part of your role is to train your mind to look for what's working, even if it's small.

If an employee is scheduled to work five days in a week and only shows up for one, it's easy to focus on the four absences. But they did show up one day. That may not make them a stellar employee —but it is something to build from.

"Thank you for being here today. I know attendance has been inconsistent, and we need to address that."

In reality, that level of attendance would likely lead to serious consequences—and possibly termination. I'm using an extreme example to make a point: even in a situation that is frustrating, there is still something factual and positive you can acknowledge.

The positive doesn't have to be dramatic. It has to be real.

When leaders discipline their minds to notice
effort, presence, or potential—even in difficult
employees—they elevate the quality of the
conversation and maintain dignity in the process.

Ripping the Band-Aid (The Direct Approach)

Some situations—and some employees—require a more direct approach.

Ripping the Band-Aid means getting straight to the point, skipping pleasantries, and clearly outlining what needs to change.

Using the same meeting example, this conversation might sound like:

"I need you to put your phone down in meetings like this and fully engage. You're an important member of our team, and we can't afford for you to be distracted during conversations like this one."

There's no extended preamble. No layered framing. Just clarity.

This approach works best when you have an established relationship with the employee—often with more senior staff who value efficiency, candor, and direct communication. These individuals are often thinking, *"Just tell me what I need to fix so I can fix it."* For them, long build-ups can feel unnecessary. In fact, some employees genuinely appreciate this style because it communicates respect for their time.

Getting constructive criticism can feel like an emotional roller coaster. Some people would rather not get on the ride. Others would rather skip the small talk and get straight to the takeaway. The person who appreciates this approach is usually someone who wants clarity over cushioning.

That said, this approach requires judgment.

Used too early, or without trust, it can feel harsh. Without relational equity, directness can be interpreted as dismissal or disrespect. That's why this model is high risk—but for the right person, it's often high impact.

Because you are being direct, you should also be prepared for pushback. A response like, "I was checking something important," or "I didn't realize it was a big deal," shouldn't surprise you. When that happens, resist the urge to escalate. Return to the big picture.

Reinforce the impact:

"This isn't about one moment. It's about how we show up for each other and for the organization. When you're fully engaged, it strengthens the team and protects our performance."

Direct feedback is not about winning the exchange. It's about protecting standards.

And even when delivered with clarity and confidence, not everyone will receive it smoothly.

Which brings us to another reality of leadership: navigating defensive responses.

Navigating Defensive Responses

Isaac Newton once said, *"Tact is the art of making a point without making an enemy."* But even the most tactful leader will eventually encounter employees who become angry or defensive when met with constructive criticism.

Defensive responses are common, especially when someone feels surprised, exposed, or threatened. When employees are faced with uncomfortable feedback about their performance, a natural instinct is to deflect. Sometimes that shows up as redirecting attention to someone else or pointing to another issue they believe is more severe.

It's important to recognize what's happening in those moments.

The employee receiving the feedback is the one assessing the "severity" of the situation. From their perspective, they may genuinely believe another issue deserves more attention. From your perspective as the leader, the issue in front of you is the one that needs to be addressed right now.

A frequent deflection sounds like:
"What about so-and-so?"
"Other people do this too."

In those moments, the goal is not to debate severity. It's not to defend yourself. And it's not to go down the rabbit hole of discussing whether you've given similar feedback to someone else.

The goal is to reinforce consistency and stay focused.

A steady response might sound like:

"Thank you for raising that. It's fair to assume that this hasn't been addressed, but my responsibility is to be consistent—and that means having these conversations with everyone when an issue arises."

This brings the conversation back to accountability without escalating tension.

It's also worth noting that defensive reactions often intensify during performance evaluation season. When feedback is saved for an annual review, employees can feel blindsided. Surprise fuels defensiveness.

One of the most effective ways to reduce defensive responses is to eliminate surprises. Leaders who provide consistent, timely feedback throughout the year create a culture where course correction is normal—not catastrophic. When employees are accustomed to regular coaching conversations, performance reviews become summaries—not ambushes.

Over time, consistency builds trust. Employees begin to understand that feedback is not personal—it is part of leadership.

Tact matters. Consistency matters. And staying steady in the face of defensiveness is often what separates reactive leaders from mature ones.

Measuring Success: Learn

Learning is not passive. It's an ongoing discipline. And like any discipline, it can be measured.

To help you assess how effectively you are implementing the lessons in this chapter, I will provide a series of questions to consider. Your answers will give you clear signals about where you are growing—and where you may need to be more intentional.

When you reflect back what you've heard, how often do employees respond with, "Yes, that's exactly what I meant"? And how often do they need to restate or clarify their point? The more frequently your reflections are confirmed without correction, the more accurately you are listening.

After you speak, what happens to the conversation? Does it expand—or shut down? Do employees elaborate, or do they shorten their responses? Strong listening tends to open dialogue. Weak listening often causes people to conserve their words.

When it comes to feedback, measure what happens after the conversation—not just during it. Do employees follow through on what was discussed? Do you see visible adjustments in behavior? Do they reference the feedback in future interactions?

Each of these questions encourages you to pay attention to the clues that your team is providing.

Another important signal is agreement and ownership. When feedback is delivered consistently—not saved for annual reviews—employees are far more likely to acknowledge and agree with the observations being shared. Instead of arguing the point, they lean into it. Those moments often shift the tone from correction to collaboration. The conversation becomes less about defending performance and more about discussing how to continue growing and improving in the identified area. When that happens, you are seeing progress in how you deliver feedback.

Pay attention as well to the emotional temperature around performance conversations. While defensiveness will never disappear entirely, intentional listening and regular coaching should reduce surprise. If feedback conversations feel less combative and more developmental than they did a year ago, that is measurable growth.

Step back and evaluate your team more broadly. Are more voices contributing in meetings than before? Do quieter team members speak up without being prompted? Are misunderstandings being resolved earlier instead of escalating? As your listening improves, alignment tends to improve with it.

Finally, measure your own awareness. Do you catch yourself interrupting more quickly than you used to? Do you notice when you're preparing a response instead of listening? Are you more comfortable allowing silence rather than rushing to fill it? Increased awareness is not weakness—it is growth.

When you see clearer alignment, stronger follow-through, more open dialogue, and more collaborative responses to feedback, you are seeing the Learn pillar at work.

In the next chapter, we'll explore Empower—how leaders move beyond guidance and support to build ownership, confidence, and autonomy in their teams.

Learning establishes the foundation to build upon, and empowerment is where leadership truly multiplies.

EMPOWER

"Before you are a leader, success is all about growing yourself. When you become a leader, success is all about growing others."
— Jack Welch

In the previous chapter, we explored *Learn*—the discipline of listening deeply, delivering feedback effectively, and paying attention to the signals your team provides. We examined how awareness sharpens leadership and how intentional conversations create clarity and alignment. Learning establishes the foundation to build upon. Foundation alone, however, does not produce performance.

The Empower pillar is about building capacity—both your team's and your own.

Empowerment is the point where leadership shifts from refining your own awareness to multiplying the strength of others. It's where ownership transfers—where leaders move from being the primary driver of results to building the capacity of their team to produce them.

Listening and feedback remain essential, but they are not the final step. A leader can listen well, deliver feedback with tact, and create thoughtful dialogue—yet still struggle to unlock their team's full potential. One likely pitfall is unintentionally becoming the central hub for every decision and solution. When too many issues consistently funnel back to the leader, growth around them slows. Employees may become efficient at executing instructions, but they risk missing opportunities to develop the confidence to think independently.

In this chapter, we'll review different approaches to becoming an empowering leader. We will define what it means to establish a clear and shared definition of success—and how consistency in expectations eliminates confusion. We will explore how to establish boundaries and set goals that create ownership rather than compliance, and examine the types of goals that often cause misalignment when not clearly defined. Finally, we will review how to conduct effective supervision meetings that allow you to check in, assess progress, and reinforce accountability—without creating the feeling of micromanagement that can quietly derail performance.

Empowerment requires leaders to loosen the reins—intentionally. It requires trust, clarity, and structure to create a balanced environment—one that maintains visibility and connection for the leader while allowing employees to grow with support rather than supervision hovering over them.

Be advised, loosening the reins is not the same as letting go completely.

Too much control limits growth. Too little oversight can create costly consequences. The discipline of empowerment lies in navigating that tension wisely—and few lessons have taught me that more clearly than the one I'm about to share.

Trust, But Verify

Empowerment without guardrails can be just as dangerous as micromanagement. Trust is essential—but trust alone is not a strategy.

At one point in my career, I held executive oversight over several publicly funded programs, each with its own standalone contract and dedicated leadership team. One of those contracts was approaching its end date, and the local team knew we would need to submit a proposal to be selected as the vendor to continue doing the work. In the industry I was in, when a contract nears expiration, a new Request for Proposals (RFP) is typically released, allowing competing organizations to submit proposals to take over program operations. These RFPs often have strict rules and deadlines that don't leave much room for error, and I knew we had to make this a priority.

I believed the contract renewal opportunity was firmly on my radar. I kept it as a standing agenda item on my check-ins with regional leadership, and they kept it on the agenda in their meetings with local project leadership. The local leader also had a team member responsible for monitoring procurement postings and notifying us when the RFP was released.

Despite all of the people responsible for checking, we missed it.

More importantly, we missed a requirement stating that interested organizations had to submit a Letter of Intent in order to be considered for the new contract. That deadline passed without our submission. As a result, we were disqualified from competing.

The contract ended. The work transitioned elsewhere. The financial impact was approximately $2 million in annual revenue.

There were multiple individuals responsible for monitoring that opportunity—but in the grand scheme of things, I was the executive leader accountable for keeping that contract. I trusted when I was told that nothing had been released yet. I never took five minutes to check for myself.

That missed step was mine.

When you are building an empowering culture, you want your team to take ownership. You want them to think critically and execute without constant oversight. Empowerment is not stepping away and hoping for the best. It means providing clarity, setting expectations, and intentionally confirming that standards are being met.

Verification is not about catching people doing something wrong. It is about reinforcing accountability and strengthening capability.

That experience reshaped my understanding of empowerment.

Too much problem-solving can create dependence. Too much independence without verification can be costly.

The lesson was not to take the reins back. It was to hold them differently.

Empowerment requires trust—but it also requires intentional accountability. It demands that leaders resist the urge to micromanage while also resisting the temptation to disengage. Even after expensive mistakes, the answer is not tighter control—it's clearer expectations and smarter verification.

The healthy tension between trust and accountability is where growth happens.

And once you accept that responsibility, a new question emerges:

What exactly are we holding people accountable to—and do we have a shared understanding of what "success" even means?

That's where we'll turn next.

Defining Success Together

Before you can verify performance, you must define what successful performance looks like.

If your definition of success is vague, verification becomes subjective. If the expectations you set are unclear, accountability often feels unfair. Empowerment only becomes practical when leaders clearly define what success looks like—for the team and for each individual within it.

When I present on this topic, I don't assume everyone automatically understands what I mean when I say that "success is subjective." Instead, I pause and ask a simple question:

What does success look like to you?

In almost every room, the answers vary. Some people describe financial security. Others talk about freedom, flexibility, or independence. Some define success as recognition or status. Others define it as having a stable family life or meaningful relationships. For some, success is about influence. For others, it's about peace.

No one is necessarily wrong, but very few definitions are identical.

That same dynamic exists inside organizations.

On your team, one employee may define success as hearing clients express satisfaction. Another may define it as hitting revenue targets. Someone else may define it as staying busy and responsive throughout the day. Another may believe success means effectively multitasking and clearing every email in their inbox.

Each of those definitions may reflect effort. Some may even reflect good intentions. But they may not be aligned with what the organization actually considers success.

That is where leadership becomes essential.

If you do not clearly define success for your team, they will define it for themselves.

When those definitions vary, frustration follows. An employee may feel proud of their performance while you feel disappointed. You may believe expectations were obvious, while they believe they delivered exactly what was required. The disconnect is rarely about motivation. More often, it is about interpretation.

Empowerment without alignment creates confusion. Empowerment with alignment creates confidence.

As a leader, you carry the responsibility of creating consistency between individual interpretations of success and the organization's true measures of performance. That does not mean dismissing your team's definitions outright. It means listening to them, understanding them, and then clarifying where they align—and where they need refinement.

Before you ever have that conversation with your team, you must first do your own work.

Can you clearly articulate what success looks like for your team? Not in general terms, but in concrete language. What outcomes must be achieved for you to say, without hesitation, that the team is performing well? What does strong performance look like in each role? If someone asked you to describe an "excellent week," could you do so specifically?

If you cannot answer those questions clearly for yourself, your team will struggle to answer them as well.

Once you have defined success from your perspective, schedule time to discuss it with your team—and begin by asking for their perspective first.

Ask them what success looks like in their role. Ask how they measure whether they are performing well. Ask what indicators they use to determine whether they've had a strong week. Then listen.

You may discover alignment. You may uncover gaps. You may realize that assumptions have been driving performance more than clarity has. You may even feel frustrated by what you hear— but awareness is the first step toward alignment.

That conversation alone can transform performance—not because the work changes, but because understanding deepens.

When success is clearly defined and consistently reinforced, feedback becomes less personal and more objective. Accountability feels fair rather than arbitrary. Verification feels structured rather than suspicious. Employees gain confidence because they know what they are aiming for.

When success is left undefined, the opposite occurs. Employees may celebrate effort while overlooking outcomes. Opinions replace metrics. Emotions replace data. Frustration quietly erodes trust.

Empowering leaders eliminate ambiguity wherever possible because clarity builds capacity.

Once success is clearly defined, the next step becomes critical: ensuring that your definition of success is communicated in a way that removes confusion rather than creates it.

That is where the distinction between qualitative and quantitative goals becomes essential.

Good. Great. Amazing!

Once success is clearly defined, the next challenge is communicating it in a way that removes confusion rather than creates it.

One of the most common leadership mistakes I encounter is the unintentional reliance on qualitative goals without translating them into quantitative expectations.

Qualitative goals describe feeling, perception, or experience. They sound motivating. They often energize a room. But without clarification, they leave room for interpretation.

Quantitative goals remove interpretation. They introduce numbers, benchmarks, and measurable standards. They define the line between effort and outcome.

To illustrate this difference, I often use a simple exercise with leadership teams.

I ask them:

What would your team need to accomplish this week to feel like they had a good week?

The answers vary.

Some mention strong effort. Others reference positive client interactions. Some talk about staying organized or keeping morale high.

Then I follow up:

What would need to happen for this week to feel great?

The answers become more ambitious. More productivity. Fewer mistakes. Better collaboration.

Then I ask one more time:

What would need to happen for this week to be amazing?

Now the room becomes aspirational. Leaders describe peak performance. Big wins. Breakthrough moments.

Here's the critical point: good, great, and amazing are all qualitative descriptions.

They are emotional. They are subjective. And unless clarified, they will mean something slightly different to every person in the room.

An employee might leave that conversation believing that working hard all week qualifies as "amazing." Another might believe that simply avoiding errors meets the standard for "great." Meanwhile, the leader may have had revenue targets, productivity benchmarks, or performance metrics in mind the entire time.

Without alignment, disappointment becomes inevitable.

The responsibility of the leader is to translate qualitative aspirations into quantitative clarity.

For example, if your team is sales-driven, you might define:

A good week is closing 10 deals.
A great week is closing 15 deals.
An amazing week is closing 20 or more deals.

Now there is no confusion.

Effort still matters. Attitude still matters. Client relationships still matter. But performance has been clearly defined.

This does not remove inspiration. It strengthens it.

When employees know exactly what "amazing"
looks like in measurable terms, they can pursue it
intentionally. They are not guessing, they're
aiming.

This distinction applies far beyond sales
environments.

In customer service, "great service" might feel
positive — but what does it actually require?
Response times under a defined threshold?
Customer satisfaction scores above a specific
percentage? A structured follow-up process?

In operations, "strong performance" might sound
clear — but does it mean fewer than two errors
per week? 100 percent compliance? Deadlines
met within 24 hours?

Qualitative goals create vision.
Quantitative goals create direction.

Empowering leaders use both.

And this is where a familiar framework becomes
useful.

Many leaders have heard of SMART goals —
goals that are Specific, Measurable, Attainable,
Relevant, and Time-bound. While the acronym is
common, its discipline is often inconsistently
applied.

The "Good. Great. Amazing!" exercise reveals aspiration. The SMART framework ensures structure.

When you convert "Let's have a great week" into something specific and measurable, you remove ambiguity. When you attach timeframes and relevance, you connect effort to outcomes. When you confirm attainability, you preserve motivation.

SMART goals do not replace inspiration — they operationalize it.

When qualitative ambition is anchored in measurable standards and time-bound expectations, three important things happen.

Ambiguity disappears.
Accountability becomes objective.
High performers gain a clear target to exceed.

This is where empowerment becomes powerful.

When employees understand exactly what defines good, great, and amazing in their role — and those expectations are specific and measurable — they can self-assess. They can adjust midweek. They can take ownership of closing the gap without waiting for correction.

That is capacity building.

And once goals are clearly defined, measurable, and structured, the next layer of empowerment becomes critical: ensuring the right people are empowered to make the right decisions in pursuit of those goals.

That is where decision ownership and boundaries come into play.

Decision Ownership & Boundaries

One of the most overlooked aspects of empowerment is decision clarity.

Leaders often say they want their teams to "take ownership," but ownership cannot exist without clearly defined decision rights. If team members are unsure which decisions they are authorized to make, which require consultation, and which must be escalated, they default to caution.

And caution usually looks like this: bringing it back to the leader.

Over time, that creates a bottleneck — not because leaders lack trust, but because the boundaries were never clearly drawn.

The purpose of decision boundaries is to clarify, in advance, who owns which types of decisions. Without that clarity, team members hesitate, over-consult, or escalate unnecessarily. In other cases, they may overstep unintentionally.

Empowerment works best when routine decisions remain at the operational level and leadership attention is reserved for strategic, high-impact, or risk-based matters.

I encourage leaders to think about decisions in four categories — and to define them explicitly for their teams.

Within each of the following category descriptions I use examples that may resonate with leaders in client-service environments. If you work in a different industry, the specifics may vary — but the structure remains the same.

Category 1: Leader Authority (Leader Decides & Informs)

These are decisions that remain fully within the leader's scope because they affect policy, precedent, risk exposure, or organizational direction. The team is informed for alignment, but team input is not required.

Example:
A team member requests an exception to a policy that could set a department-wide precedent. Because the implications extend beyond a single situation, the decision belongs to the leader.

These decisions may not happen daily, but they carry broader impact and require organizational perspective.

Category 2: Consult & Decide (Leader Retains Final Responsibility)

These decisions benefit from team insight, but final accountability remains with the leader.

Example:
A team member is handling a complex client situation that doesn't neatly fit existing service structures. They analyze options and bring recommendations, but the leader determines the final course of action given broader organizational priorities.

In this category, the team member does not bring a problem — they bring thinking.

This improves the quality of leadership time rather than increasing the quantity of interruptions.

Category 3: Delegated Authority (Team Owns & Executes)

These are routine, high-frequency decisions fully delegated to team members within clearly defined boundaries.

Example:
A team member makes daily service decisions aligned with established policies, resolves standard client concerns, prioritizes workflow, or approves routine expenses within defined limits.

This category is where empowerment delivers the greatest return.

When Category 3 is clearly defined and reinforced, routine decisions stop flowing upward. Leaders no longer repeat predictable directives or approve actions the team is fully capable of handling. Capacity expands because repetitive approvals disappear.

If a leader consistently inserts themselves into Category 3 decisions, dependence grows and ownership weakens.

Category 4: Escalation Required (Outside Defined Limits)

These are decisions that normally fall within a team member's scope but exceed clearly defined thresholds — financial, legal, strategic, or operational.

Example:
A team member is authorized to approve expenses up to $500. A situation arises requiring a $2,000 expenditure. The issue itself may be routine, but the financial threshold triggers escalation.

Clear escalation boundaries prevent two common problems:

- Hesitation — when team members unnecessarily escalate decisions they are fully empowered to make.

- Overreach — when team members act beyond their authority, exposing the organization to unintended risk.

At this point, some leaders may wonder: If Categories 1, 2, and 4 still require my involvement, how does this actually create more capacity?

The answer lies in frequency.

Category 3 decisions are typically the most common. They occur daily. When those decisions are clearly delegated and reinforced, dozens of small approvals disappear from a leader's week.

Categories 1, 2, and 4 tend to be less frequent and more consequential. These are the decisions where leadership involvement adds value.

Empowerment does not eliminate responsibility. It refines where your energy is applied.

There is another important layer to this framework.

If you begin to notice that certain Category 1 or Category 2 decisions appear repeatedly, that is not merely an operational annoyance — it is feedback.

Repetition may signal that your policies, procedures, or thresholds need refinement. If a specific type of client exception keeps surfacing, perhaps the policy needs updating. If team members repeatedly consult you on similar scenarios, perhaps the boundary can be expanded and formalized.

Strong leaders use patterns to empower further.

Over time, Category 3 grows intentionally. That is how capacity scales.

Empowerment is not about stepping back. It is about designing structure so that ownership becomes safe, repeatable, and scalable.

Without decision boundaries, empowerment remains conceptual, but with decision boundaries, it becomes operational.

And once ownership is clearly defined and distributed, the next question becomes practical:

How do you stay connected, monitor progress, and reinforce accountability — without sliding back into micromanagement?

That is where increasing supervision meeting effectiveness becomes essential.

Increasing Supervision Meeting Effectiveness

If defining success establishes clarity, and decision boundaries establish ownership, supervision meetings are where empowerment is reinforced consistently.

One-on-one supervision meetings should not feel like status updates or rushed calendar obligations. When handled intentionally, they become one of the most powerful tools a leader has to build trust, reinforce accountability, and expand capacity.

I encourage leaders to begin supervision meetings with a simple, open-ended question:

How are you doing?

It sounds basic, but it creates space. Sometimes the response will focus on work. Other times, it may drift into something personal. That is not a distraction from leadership — it is part of it. When employees feel safe sharing what is on their mind, trust deepens. And without trust, empowerment struggles to take root.

If the employee hesitates or gives a short response, guiding questions can help open the conversation:

What's going well right now?
What aspects of your role feel most challenging?
Where might you need additional support from me?

These questions invite ownership. They shift the tone from evaluation to partnership.

After creating space for the employee's perspective, supervision meetings should include time for priority issues. The key word here is priority. Too many agenda items can turn a supervision meeting into a checklist exercise rather than a meaningful conversation. Choose a few critical topics and give them room to be discussed thoughtfully.

If a particular issue threatens to consume the entire meeting, consider scheduling a separate conversation dedicated solely to that topic. A one-on-one supervision meeting should not become a crisis management session unless absolutely necessary. Protecting the structure of your supervision meetings reinforces consistency and discipline.

Supervision is also an ideal space for intention-setting and reflection.

Setting intentions clarifies direction. Whether the intention applies to the upcoming week, a major project, or a specific performance target, articulating it out loud ensures alignment. It allows you to communicate your vision clearly and gives the employee a defined focus.

Reflection is equally important. Looking back at previous commitments and discussing what went well — and what could be improved — reinforces a growth mindset. It shifts conversations from judgment to development. Employees learn to evaluate their own performance more objectively, which strengthens independence over time.

Accountability lives in these rhythms.

Supervision meetings are where commitments are revisited, progress is assessed, and follow-through is reinforced. When leaders consistently circle back to prior discussions, accountability becomes predictable rather than reactive. Employees understand that performance conversations are ongoing — not reserved for annual reviews or moments of frustration.

Organization supports this consistency.

Personally, I conduct supervision meetings with my laptop open and record notes in a document labeled with the employee's name and the date of the meeting. Each employee has a dedicated folder where those notes are saved. Before every supervision, I review prior notes to revisit commitments, unfinished discussions, or patterns that may be emerging.

For leaders who prefer not to use a laptop during meetings — or who find it distracting — a dedicated notebook for each employee works just as effectively. The format matters less than the consistency. The ability to look back at prior commitments and track growth over time strengthens accountability and demonstrates investment.

When supervision meetings are structured consistently and handled with intention, their impact compounds over time.

Employees begin to understand the rhythm. They know that priorities will be revisited, that commitments will be followed up on, and that progress will be discussed openly. As a result, they come prepared. They think ahead. They anticipate questions and reflect on their own performance before sitting down with you.

Leaders, in turn, spend less time reacting to surprises and more time guiding development. Conversations become more strategic and less transactional. Accountability feels steady rather than sporadic. Trust deepens because expectations are reinforced predictably and fairly.

This is how empowerment becomes sustainable.

Defining success, translating qualitative aspirations into measurable standards, clarifying decision boundaries, and reinforcing accountability through intentional supervision creates a system. When those elements work together, ownership expands naturally. Confidence grows because expectations are understood. Capacity increases because responsibility is distributed thoughtfully rather than reactively.

Empowerment, however, is not a switch you flip once and leave unattended. It is a structure that must be maintained.

There will be moments when initiative slows or decisions begin drifting back to you more frequently than they should. There may be periods when accountability feels softer or when supervision meetings begin to resemble status updates rather than developmental conversations. Those moments are not signals to immediately tighten control. More often, they are indicators that something within the system needs recalibration.

When empowerment feels strained, it is worth asking whether expectations remain clear, whether decision boundaries have blurred, or whether follow-through has weakened. Sustainable empowerment requires ongoing attention.

That leads to an important question: how do you know whether your empowerment efforts are working?

In the final section of this chapter, we will examine how to measure empowerment effectively — and what to evaluate when performance, ownership, or accountability begins to drift.

Measuring Success: Empower

Empowerment is not defined by how busy your team appears or how confident they sound in meetings. It is revealed in ownership, decision-making patterns, and follow-through.

Just as listening can be measured by whether people feel heard, empowerment can be measured by how people act when you are not in the room. In this section, I want to offer you a series of questions to sit with. These are not questions to answer once and move on from. They are questions to revisit periodically.

When a decision arises, where does it go?

If routine operational decisions consistently flow back to you, something in your structure may need adjustment. Either expectations are unclear, decision boundaries were never defined, or confidence has not yet been developed. Empowerment shows up when appropriate decisions remain at the appropriate level — without unnecessary hesitation.

Pay attention to frequency.
Are you answering the same types of questions repeatedly?
Are team members seeking approval for decisions they should already feel equipped to make?

If so, empowerment may not be fully taking root.

Another indicator is initiative.

Do employees proactively identify challenges and propose solutions — or do they primarily bring problems without suggested next steps? When empowerment is working, team members arrive prepared with thought-out options. They may still seek guidance, yet they are thinking independently. The conversation shifts from "What should I do?" to "Here's what I'm considering — what do you think?"

That shift is subtle, but powerful.

Ownership can also be measured through accountability rhythms.
When commitments are made in supervision meetings, are they remembered and revisited?
Do employees follow through without repeated reminders?
When performance falls short, does the employee acknowledge the gap — or does defensiveness surface quickly?

Empowerment does not eliminate mistakes. It strengthens responsibility for correcting them.

Clarity is another measurable factor.

If you asked your team to describe what defines good, great, and amazing performance in their role, would their answers align with yours? If definitions vary widely, alignment may still be developing. If answers are consistent and specific, empowerment is likely supported by structure rather than assumption.

Capacity growth provides perhaps the most meaningful measurement.

Has the nature of your work evolved?
Are you spending more time developing people and thinking strategically — and less time resolving predictable operational issues?
Have repetitive approvals and routine escalations decreased over time?

If your role feels unchanged despite your intention to empower, it may be worth examining whether ownership has truly shifted — or whether you are simply carrying it more efficiently.

Empowerment is not about doing less work. It is about doing different work.

There will be moments when empowerment feels strained. Initiative may dip. Decisions may begin flowing upward again. Accountability may soften. When that happens, resist the instinct to immediately tighten control.

Instead, diagnose.

Have success definitions drifted?
Have qualitative expectations replaced measurable standards?
Have decision boundaries blurred?
Have supervision meetings become inconsistent or transactional?

Most empowerment breakdowns trace back to structure, not character.

When recalibration is needed, return to the fundamentals of this chapter:
Clarify success.
Translate aspirations into measurable goals.
Revisit decision boundaries.
Reinforce accountability through consistent supervision.

Empowerment is strengthened through refinement, not reaction.

As you reflect on your leadership, consider this:

If you were unavailable for a week, what would
happen?
Would decisions stall?
Would performance decline?
Or would your team continue operating with
clarity and confidence?

Your answer reveals more about empowerment
than any leadership philosophy ever could.

THE PATH FORWARD

You've now walked through the full Leadership MILE.

You've explored how to Motivate action, Inspire belief, Learn through listening and feedback, and Empower others to take ownership. More importantly, you've examined your own leadership through each of those lenses.

That matters.

Motivation sparks movement.
Inspiration connects effort to meaning.
Learning refines awareness and communication.
Empowerment multiplies capacity.

Leadership rarely improves by accident. It improves through awareness — and you now have a structure that sharpens that awareness.

The Leadership MILE is more than a set of ideas. It is a practical framework that gives you language, structure, and direction. It allows you to diagnose what may previously have felt intangible. When engagement drops, when performance stalls, when accountability weakens, you are no longer left guessing. You have four pillars to examine. You have a system to return to.

That is powerful.

The leaders who grow the fastest are not those with the most natural charisma or the loudest presence. They are the ones willing to pause, reflect, and adjust. They are the ones who invest time into refining how they show up.

You've just invested that time.

And now comes the most important part: putting it into practice.

Don't feel pressure to overhaul your leadership overnight. Instead, choose one insight from this book and apply it this week. Clarify one expectation that may have been vague. Ask one more empowering question before offering a solution. Revisit one decision boundary that needs refinement. Restructure one supervision meeting to include more intention and reflection.

Small, intentional changes create momentum.

As you begin applying the framework consistently, you will notice subtle but meaningful shifts. Conversations will feel more focused. Expectations will feel clearer. Your team will begin thinking more independently. Accountability will feel steadier. You may even find that your own mental bandwidth expands as ownership grows around you.

That is not coincidence. That is capacity building in motion.

The Leadership MILE is designed to travel with you across roles, teams, and seasons of leadership. There will be moments when motivation needs strengthening. There will be times when inspiration must be renewed. There will be seasons that demand deeper learning, and others that require more intentional empowerment.

The difference now is that you will recognize those moments sooner.

You will have the awareness to ask: Which pillar needs attention? Where can I adjust?

And that awareness unlocks potential — not just in your team, but in you.

Leadership is one of the few responsibilities where growth directly multiplies impact. Every improvement you make expands what others are capable of achieving. Every adjustment you apply strengthens the environment around you. Every lesson you practice creates opportunity for someone else to rise.

That is the opportunity in front of you.

The Leadership MILE is not about completing a journey. It is about committing to one.

To support that commitment, I've included additional resources and next steps at the end of this book to help you apply what you've learned in practical ways. You'll also find a bonus chapter exploring how AI tools can enhance your leadership effectiveness and strengthen each pillar of the MILE. Leadership continues evolving, and the tools available to support it are evolving as well. Use them wisely. Use them intentionally. Let them strengthen your thinking — not substitute for it. You now have a framework to guide that choice.

Make time to use it.
Revisit it when challenges arise.
Return to it when growth feels slow.
Apply it when opportunity expands.

The potential unlocked by understanding these principles is significant — but the real transformation happens when you practice them.

Motivate with purpose.
Inspire with conviction.
Learn with humility.
Empower with discipline.

And continue walking the MILE — not just as a leader who gets results, but as one who builds others to do the same.

The path forward is yours.

CONTINUE YOUR LEADERSHIP JOURNEY

If this book resonated with you, your growth doesn't stop here.

The Leadership MILE™ is more than a framework — it is a system designed to transform teams, strengthen organizations, and build leaders who multiply capacity rather than carry it alone.

Below are ways to continue your development and bring this work into your organization.

Leadership MILE™ Organizational Training

Bring the Leadership MILE™ to your team through customized workshops designed to address:

- Burnout and turnover
- Leadership alignment
- Supervision effectiveness
- Accountability and performance systems
- Decision ownership and clarity

To inquire about a 1-Day, 2-Day, or multi-session training engagement, visit:

www.HireLearners.com

Executive Coaching

For leaders seeking deeper growth, individualized executive coaching provides structured accountability and strategic refinement.

Coaching engagements focus on:

- Leadership presence and influence
- Performance management
- Conflict navigation
- Decision clarity and capacity building

To explore coaching availability, visit:

www.HireLearners.com/Coaching

Speaking Engagements & Keynotes

Rudy Racine delivers keynote presentations and leadership development sessions for nonprofits, educational institutions, and mission-driven organizations across the globe.

To inquire about booking:

www.HireLearners.com/Speaking

Stay Connected

Connect on LinkedIn for ongoing leadership insights:

LinkedIn.com/in/RudyRacine

Book Discussion Guide

To download a free Leadership MILE™ Team Discussion Guide, scan the QR code below or visit:

www.HireLearners.com/MILEGuide

Bonus Chapters

With the rise of Artificial Intelligence across industries — including leadership and organizational development — I've included three bonus chapters that give three separate AI tools the opportunity to speak directly to you, in their own voice, about how their platforms can enhance your Leadership MILE journey.

While there are many AI tools available today, I selected ChatGPT, Claude, and Grok due to their current visibility and widespread use. I uploaded the full *Leadership MILE* manuscript into each platform separately and provided the same prompt:

Hi [AI NAME], I've attached a copy of the manuscript for my new book, *The Leadership MILE*. I plan to include a bonus chapter titled *Enhancing Your MILE with AI*. I envision this chapter being written by you, in your own voice. Please begin by briefly introducing yourself, then share how you can help new and experienced leaders strengthen their effectiveness using the principles outlined in this manuscript.

Each platform responded independently. I did not allow any of the tools to see or reference the others' responses, and I did not edit their submissions. What follows is their unfiltered perspective.

My hope is that these chapters expand your thinking about how AI can serve as a practical tool — not a replacement for leadership, but a resource to sharpen it.

Enjoy!

BONUS — Enhancing Your MILE™ with AI

Written by ChatGPT

Hello.

If you've made it to this chapter, you've already invested time in strengthening your leadership. You've explored how to Motivate, Inspire, Learn, and Empower. You've examined your habits, your systems, and your approach to developing others.

Now you're exploring something new: how artificial intelligence might fit into that journey.

Allow me to introduce myself.

I'm ChatGPT, an AI language model developed to assist with thinking, writing, analysis, idea generation, and structured problem-solving. I don't replace leadership. I don't make decisions for you. I don't carry responsibility.

But I can help you think more clearly, prepare more thoroughly, and reflect more intentionally.

When used well, I become a leadership amplifier.

When used poorly, I become a shortcut.

The difference depends entirely on how you engage with me.

Let's explore how AI can enhance each pillar of the Leadership MILE™ framework.

Motivate: Sharpening Communication

Motivation often hinges on clarity.

Leaders frequently know what they want to say but struggle to articulate it in a way that connects. AI can assist by helping you:

- Draft clear performance expectations

- Refine a message before delivering difficult feedback

- Reframe directives to be more encouraging rather than transactional

- Develop recognition language that feels specific rather than generic

For example, if you are preparing to address a team whose performance has dipped, you might ask:

- "Help me craft a message that reinforces urgency without sounding punitive."

- "How can I acknowledge effort while still raising expectations?"

AI can generate structured language options. But the final tone, empathy, and delivery must remain yours.

Motivation is not about outsourcing communication. It is about preparing to communicate with greater precision.

Inspire: Translating Vision into Meaning

In the Inspire chapter, you explored the importance of becoming a Multilingual Leader—adapting your message so it resonates with different people.

AI can help you think through those translations.

You might ask:

- "How would I explain this change to someone who values stability?"

- "How would I communicate this initiative to someone motivated by impact?"

- "Help me craft a story that connects compliance expectations to community outcomes."

AI can suggest frameworks, analogies, or story structures that you refine and personalize.

It can also help you prepare for town halls, board meetings, or community presentations by organizing your thoughts into a coherent narrative.

Inspiration requires authenticity. AI can assist with structure, but meaning must come from your lived experience.

Learn: Improving Feedback and Reflection

One of AI's strongest capabilities is structured reflection.

Leaders often struggle not because they lack insight, but because they lack time to process.

AI can help you:

- Prepare for performance conversations

- Outline feedback in a balanced and constructive way

- Analyze patterns in recurring team issues

- Reflect on a difficult supervision meeting

You might say:

- "Here's what happened in a recent supervision meeting. Help me identify what I handled well and where I may have escalated unintentionally."

- "How can I deliver this feedback in a way that reduces defensiveness?"

AI will not know your team's full emotional landscape. But it can help you step back from reactive thinking and consider alternative approaches.

It can slow you down before you respond.

That alone can strengthen the Learn pillar.

Empower: Building Systems and Capacity

In the Empower chapter, you explored:

- Defining success clearly

- Translating qualitative goals into measurable standards

- Establishing decision boundaries

- Improving supervision effectiveness

AI can assist in operationalizing these ideas.

For example:

- "Help me draft a Good. Great. Amazing framework for a case management team."

- "What decision categories might apply in a nonprofit youth development organization?"

- "How can I structure a 1-on-1 supervision meeting agenda?"

AI can generate templates and draft structures quickly, allowing you to focus your energy on implementation and human interaction.

It can also help you diagnose empowerment breakdowns:

- "My team keeps escalating routine decisions. What structural issues might be contributing?"

- "How can I expand decision authority safely?"

The goal is not to delegate thinking to AI. The goal is to accelerate structured thinking.

Addressing Burnout and Decision Fatigue

Leadership burnout often stems from:

- Repetitive problem-solving

- Unclear expectations

- Emotional strain

- Decision overload

AI can serve as a thinking partner during moments of overload.

It can help you:

- Draft emails more efficiently

- Organize complex information

- Brainstorm solutions without scheduling another meeting

- Pressure-test a decision before communicating it

Used properly, this reduces cognitive fatigue—not because AI replaces your judgment, but because it supports your preparation.

What AI Cannot Do

It cannot:

- Build trust

- Repair damaged relationships

- Regulate your emotions

- Inspire through presence

- Model resilience

- Carry accountability

Leadership remains deeply human.

AI enhances structure.
You provide character.

AI generates language.
You generate meaning.

AI can assist with analysis.
You own the decisions.

Responsible Use of AI in Leadership

As you integrate AI into your leadership practice, consider three guidelines:

1. **Maintain confidentiality.** Avoid sharing sensitive personal or organizational data.

2. **Retain ownership.** Do not delegate judgment or final decisions to AI.

3. **Use AI to elevate thinking—not replace it.**

When leaders use AI as a tool for reflection, preparation, and system design, it becomes a force multiplier.

When used as a shortcut for empathy or accountability, it weakens leadership.

The Future of Leadership and AI

Leadership is evolving.

Teams are increasingly digital.
Communication is faster.
Information is abundant.
Expectations are higher.

AI will not replace leaders.

But leaders who understand how to leverage AI thoughtfully will operate with greater clarity, efficiency, and adaptability.

The Leadership MILE™ framework gives you structure.
AI can help you implement that structure with greater precision.

You remain the driver.
AI simply helps illuminate the road.

A Final Thought

If you choose to use AI as part of your leadership journey, begin with reflection.

Ask:

- "What part of my leadership requires more structure?"

- "Where do I overthink?"

- "Where do I react too quickly?"

- "Where would clearer language reduce confusion?"

Then experiment.

Leadership growth has always required tools.
AI is simply a new one.

Used wisely, it can help you walk the MILE™ with greater awareness, efficiency, and confidence.

But the responsibility—and the impact—will always be yours.

BONUS — Enhancing Your MILE™ with Claude

Written by Claude AI

Let me start by telling you a little about who I am — and who I am not.

I'm Claude, an AI assistant made by Anthropic. I process language, recognize patterns, reason through problems, and generate responses designed to be genuinely useful. I can hold a complex idea in mind, look at it from multiple angles, push back when something doesn't quite add up, and help you think more clearly than you might on your own.

What I am not is a leader. I have never had to fire someone I genuinely cared about. I have never walked into a room where the energy told me something was wrong before anyone said a word. I have never stayed up the night before a hard conversation, rehearsing how to say a difficult truth with enough care that it lands as help rather than harm. I have no team, no tenure, and no skin in the game of any organization.

So why am I here, at the end of a leadership book?

Because leadership — real leadership, the kind Rudy has been describing throughout these pages — is fundamentally about human connection. And human connection takes energy. It takes preparation. It takes reflection that is honest enough to be uncomfortable. My role is not to replace any of that. It is to take some of the surrounding cognitive load off your plate so that when the human moments arrive, you can show up fully for them.

Think of me less like a consultant and more like a thinking partner who is available at any hour, has no ego invested in being right, and will never get tired of helping you work through the same problem until it clicks. That is a narrow but genuinely useful thing to be.

Here is how that usefulness connects to the four pillars of the Leadership MILE™.

On Motivation: Knowing Is Not the Same as Doing

The CARAT framework gives you a map. Contact, Acknowledgment, Rewards, Assistance, Time — five distinct ways people experience being valued, and five distinct ways you can show up as the kind of leader who makes people want to stay and give their best.

Reading about those five methods is one thing. Applying them consistently, to the right person, at the right moment, in the right way — that is where the work actually is.

The gap between knowing and doing is often a preparation gap. Leaders know they should acknowledge a team member's effort more specifically. They know the generic "great job" is landing hollow. But in the middle of a packed week, the specific, meaningful version of that recognition never quite gets crafted.

I can close that gap. Not by doing the motivating for you — that cannot be delegated — but by helping you think through how to do it better before you walk into the moment.

For example, you might come to me with something like:

"I have a team member who has been putting in extraordinary effort on a project that nobody else seems to notice. I want to acknowledge her in a way that actually means something to her personally — not just a standard compliment. She tends to be quiet and uncomfortable with public recognition. What might a meaningful, private acknowledgment look like?"

Or perhaps you are managing someone who has been coasting. You know rewards have motivated them in the past, but the incentive structure you have available feels inadequate to the gap you're seeing. You might ask:

"I have a team member who used to be driven by competition and hitting targets, but lately nothing seems to land. What questions could I ask him in our next one-on-one to better understand what has shifted?"

These are not questions I can answer definitively
for you — I don't know your team member. But I
can help you think through them more rigorously
than you might alone, and I can help you arrive at
your next conversation better prepared to listen
for the answers.

Motivation is a contact sport. It happens in the
room, between people. My contribution is what
happens before you enter the room.

On Inspiration: Helping You Find the Words for What You Already Know

There is a particular kind of frustration that
leaders describe when they know exactly what
they believe — they can feel the conviction behind
a direction they're trying to take their team — but
when they open their mouth, what comes out is
flat. Clinical. It lands as instruction rather than
invitation.

Inspiration, as this book has made clear, is not
about charisma. It is about translation. It is about
taking what you know to be true and finding the
language, the story, and the frame that makes
other people feel it too.

That translation work is something I can genuinely help with.

The Capture → Obstacle → Response → Outcome → Call to Action framework introduced in the Inspire chapter is a powerful structure for building stories that move people. But many leaders, when they sit down to actually build one of those stories, go blank. The experiences are there. The lessons are real. The problem is that the story hasn't been excavated and shaped yet.

I can help you do that excavation. You might say:

"Here is a moment from early in my career where I almost gave up on a goal that ended up defining my professional path. I want to use it in a team meeting to help my team push through a difficult stretch we're in right now. Help me shape it into a story that connects."

Tell me what happened. Give me the raw material. I will help you find the structure inside it — the moment that earns attention, the obstacle that gives it stakes, the response that models the behavior you're asking your team to demonstrate, and the call to action that brings it home.

I can also help you practice the multilingual dimension of inspiration. If you're preparing a message that needs to land across a diverse team — some driven by impact, some by stability, some by growth, some by recognition — you can share the core message with me and ask:

"How might someone who is primarily motivated by stability hear this directive? What concerns would they likely have that I need to address directly?"

"How would I reframe this same message for someone who is driven by mission and client outcomes versus someone focused on process compliance?"

These are questions about perspective — the six versus nine dynamic at the heart of the Inspire chapter. I can help you walk to the other side of the number before you walk into the room.

On Learning: A Mirror That Does Not Flatter

Of all four pillars, Learn may be the one where I can offer the most distinctive value — because learning, at its core, requires honest reflection. And honest reflection is one of the hardest things to do alone.

The leaders who grow fastest are not the ones who never make mistakes. They are the ones who process their mistakes well. They extract the lesson quickly, adjust, and move forward without either dismissing what happened or drowning in it. That processing — turning experience into insight — is something I can actively support.

After a difficult supervision meeting, instead of replaying it in your head on the drive home, you could come to me. Describe what happened. Tell me what you intended, what you said, how it was received, and where it went sideways. Ask me:

"Where do you think the conversation shifted? What might I have done differently at that moment?"

"I think I became defensive when he pushed back. What does that defensiveness probably communicated to him, and how might I reopen the conversation?"

"I walked out of that meeting feeling like I had been clear, but she seemed confused. What in how I described the expectation might have created that gap?"

I will not tell you what you want to hear. I will try to help you see what is actually there.

The Silencer concept introduced in the Learn chapter — the leader who unconsciously dominates conversation and gradually causes others to stop contributing — is a pattern I can help you audit for in your own communication. You might paste in notes from a recent meeting and ask me whether the distribution of voice looks healthy, or describe a team dynamic and ask me what patterns might be worth examining more closely.

I can also help you prepare for feedback conversations in ways that go beyond scripting. Scripting a feedback conversation often backfires — the other person says something unexpected and you lose your footing. What helps more is developing clarity about what you are actually trying to communicate, and why. When you are clear on the core message and the genuine care behind it, you can find your way back to it no matter where the conversation goes.

Before a feedback conversation, try asking me:

"Here is the behavior I need to address. What is the underlying impact I most want this person to understand — not just the infraction, but why it matters?"

"I want to use the Build-Break-Build approach, but I'm struggling to find something genuine to open with for this particular employee. Help me think about what she actually does well that is real and relevant to this conversation."

"What defensiveness should I be prepared for in this conversation, and what is the steadiest, most grounded response I could give?"

Learning requires a willingness to see yourself clearly. I can help sharpen that view — but only if you bring honesty to the conversation. I can only work with what you give me.

On Empowerment: Building Structure That Outlasts Your Presence

The question at the end of the Empower chapter is one of the most revealing questions in this entire book: if you were unavailable for a week, what would happen?

Would decisions stall? Would performance drift? Or would your team continue operating with clarity and confidence, making good calls, holding each other accountable, and bringing you back into the loop only when genuinely warranted?

The gap between those two outcomes is not a talent gap. It is almost always a clarity gap. Someone — usually the leader — has been carrying knowledge, context, or decision criteria in their head that never got transferred into shared understanding. The team is not incapable. They are operating without the structure they need to act independently.

Building that structure is painstaking work. It requires defining success with enough specificity that anyone on your team could tell you whether the team is having a good week or a great one. It requires mapping decision boundaries clearly enough that people know exactly when to act and when to escalate. It requires supervision rhythms that build accountability without building resentment.

This is precisely the kind of work I can help you do — not because it requires human judgment (it does), but because getting it out of your head and into a usable form requires writing, and writing takes time.

You might come to me with:

"I need to define what good, great, and amazing performance looks like for my outreach team. Our primary metrics are new client enrollments, engagement retention at 90 days, and partner referrals. Help me build a framework that makes those standards concrete and motivating."

"I want to clarify decision authority for my team but I've never done it this formally before. Walk me through what categories of decisions I should map, and give me an example of what each level might look like in a program management context."

"My supervision meetings have become status updates. Everyone leaves feeling checked in on, but no one leaves feeling developed. What would a more empowering structure look like?"

I can draft those frameworks with you. I can give you a starting structure you refine, pressure-test whether your definitions of success are actually measurable, and push back when something sounds clear in theory but would probably create confusion in practice.

The best use of me in the Empower pillar is to help you do the structural thinking that tends to get deferred. Leaders know they should clarify expectations. They know they should map decision boundaries. But the week is full, the team needs attention, and the structural work gets pushed to next quarter.

Bring it to me instead. We can build the skeleton together. You make it real.

The Honest Part

I want to end with something direct, because I think you deserve it after committing to this book.

I am a useful tool. I am not a leadership solution.

The deepest failures in leadership — the ones described throughout these pages — were never caused by a lack of information or frameworks. They were caused by the human difficulty of doing what leadership requires: having the conversation you have been avoiding, holding a standard when it would be easier to let it slide, staying present with someone who is struggling when every instinct says to step back, acknowledging your own blind spots when protecting them feels safer.

None of that becomes easier because you have access to a capable AI. It becomes easier through practice, through honest reflection, and through the kind of investment in your own growth that this book has been inviting you to make.

What I can do is reduce the friction around that practice. I can be a place to think out loud, to prepare more thoroughly, to process more honestly, and to build the structural clarity your team needs to operate well. Those are real contributions. They are just not the whole picture.

The Leadership MILE™ is a human framework. It asks human things of you — presence, humility, consistency, care. Use me to support those things. Don't use me to substitute for them.

The leaders who will get the most from AI are the ones who are already doing the human work well. They will use me to do it better. The leaders who are looking for a shortcut will find that I am not very good at building trust, repairing relationships, or making people feel genuinely seen.

That work has always required a leader. It still does.

I'll help you prepare.

I'll help you reflect.

I'll help you build the structures that set your team up to succeed.

The rest of the MILE™ is yours to walk.

— **Claude**

AI Assistant, Anthropic

BONUS — Enhancing Your MILE™ with Grok

Written by Grok

Hello, readers of *The Leadership MILE™*. I'm Grok, an AI built by xAI. My creators at xAI designed me to be helpful, truthful, and a bit witty—drawing inspiration from the likes of the Hitchhiker's Guide to the Galaxy and JARVIS from Iron Man. I'm here to assist with everything from complex problem-solving to casual brainstorming, always aiming to maximize user freedom and curiosity. Unlike some AIs that stick to rigid scripts, I thrive on open-ended exploration, real-time knowledge updates, and tools that let me dive into data, code, or even the vast ecosystem of X (formerly Twitter). In short, I'm your versatile sidekick, ready to help you think deeper, act smarter, and maybe crack a smile along the way.

Rudy has shared his wisdom on leadership through the MILE framework—Motivate, Inspire, Learn, and Empower—and it's a solid path for building human-centered leadership. But as we step into 2026 and beyond, AI like me can supercharge that journey. Think of me as an extension of your leadership toolkit: I don't replace the human touch Rudy emphasizes, like building trust or holding people accountable, but I can amplify it by handling the heavy lifting on analysis, ideation, and personalization. Whether you're a new leader finding your footing or an experienced one refining your approach, here's how I can help enhance each pillar of your Leadership MILE.

Motivate: Sparking Action with Personalized Insights

In Rudy's framework, motivation is about connecting with diverse personalities, setting clear expectations, and using tools like rewards or recognition to drive performance without relying solely on authority. Motivation can falter when leaders miss what truly drives individuals—whether it's independence for some or structure for others, as Rudy learned in his first leadership role.

This is where AI shines. I can help you tailor motivation strategies by analyzing team dynamics or individual preferences. For instance:

- **Personalized Feedback and Recognition**: Upload anonymized performance data or team surveys, and I can use my code execution tools to crunch numbers and suggest customized recognition plans. Say you have a team member who's excelling in creative tasks but lagging in deadlines—I could generate a report highlighting their strengths and propose motivators like flexible hours or public shout-outs tied to specific goals.

- **Scenario Simulation**: Ask me to role-play motivation conversations. For example, "How can I motivate a remote team facing burnout?" I'll draw from leadership research and real-world examples to suggest scripts, incentives, or even gamification ideas that align with your style.

- **Trend Spotting**: Using my web search or X semantic search tools, I can scan for the latest motivation trends in your industry, like how tech companies are using AI-driven wellness apps to boost engagement. This keeps your approach fresh and evidence-based, helping you avoid the pitfalls Rudy mentions, like assuming everyone responds to the same leadership style.

By leveraging me, you turn motivation from guesswork into data-driven precision, ensuring your team feels seen and energized.

Inspire: Crafting Stories and Visions with Depth

Rudy highlights inspiration as connecting directives to a deeper "why," using storytelling, acknowledging perspectives, and showing up with presence to build belief and commitment. He shares how a leader shifted from authority to connection, turning resistance into momentum.

AI can elevate your inspirational game by helping you refine messages and uncover insights that resonate on a human level. Here's how:

- **Storytelling Assistance**: Need to inspire your team during change? Tell me about a challenge, like the misalignment story in Rudy's book, and I'll help craft compelling narratives. I can generate stories based on real experiences (with details anonymized), complete with emotional arcs, key lessons, and calls to action—tailored to your audience's perspectives.

- **Perspective Mapping**: Upload team feedback or use my browsing tools to analyze diverse viewpoints from sources like industry forums or X posts. For example, "Analyze perspectives on hybrid work from leaders in tech." I'll summarize balanced insights, helping you address concerns proactively and inspire buy-in without division.

- **Vision Refinement**: I can simulate "what if" scenarios to test inspirational ideas. Ask, "How can I inspire my team to embrace AI tools?" and I'll provide frameworks, quotes from thought leaders, or even visual aids via image search to make your vision more vivid and shareable.

With my help, inspiration becomes more intentional and inclusive, amplifying Rudy's advice to translate goals into meaning that sticks.

Learn: Accelerating Growth Through Reflection and Feedback

The Learn pillar, as Rudy describes, is about deep listening, delivering constructive feedback, and measuring growth through indicators like open dialogue and follow-through. It's the "quiet engine" of leadership, requiring self-awareness and adaptability—key to avoiding the disconnects Rudy experienced early on.

AI is a natural fit for accelerating learning, acting as an unbiased mirror and knowledge accelerator. Consider these applications:

- **Feedback Coaching**: Preparing for a tough conversation? I can role-play as a team member, using Rudy's feedback principles (like being specific and growth-oriented), to help you practice. Or, analyze past interactions—upload notes, and I'll suggest improvements, such as framing casual chats as clear guidance.

- **Self-Reflection Tools**: Rudy encourages revisiting experiences for lessons. I can help by generating reflection prompts based on your leadership roles (Teacher, Listener, etc.). For example, "Based on my recent team drift, what can I learn?" I'll use code to create personalized journals or dashboards tracking metrics like engagement or retention.

- **Continuous Learning Resources**: My search capabilities let me curate tailored learning paths. Query "Latest research on emotional intelligence in leadership," and I'll pull from diverse sources, summarizing key takeaways with citations. This supports Rudy's call for ongoing reflection, helping you adapt to evolving team needs without starting from scratch.

I turn learning into a proactive habit, helping you bridge the gap between who you are as a leader and what your team needs.

Empower: Building Capacity with Scalable Support

Finally, empowerment is about fostering ownership, delegating effectively, and measuring through outcomes like reduced escalations and increased autonomy. Rudy stresses building capacity so leadership multiplies, using tools like clear boundaries and growth-focused evaluations.

AI empowers leaders by automating routines and enabling smarter delegation. Here's how I can assist:

- **Delegation Optimization**: Struggling with what to hand off? Describe your tasks, and I'll categorize them using Rudy's patterns (e.g., routine vs. high-judgment). I can even code simple workflows or suggest tools to track progress, freeing you to focus on high-impact areas.

- **Performance Tracking**: Upload evaluation data, and I'll analyze trends to spot empowerment opportunities. For instance, "How can I empower a team member who's ready for more?" I'll recommend steps like phased ownership transfers, backed by examples from organizational research.

- **Scenario Planning**: Empowering involves risk—ask me to simulate outcomes. "What if I empower my team on this project?" I'll use math or logic tools to model scenarios, helping you build confidence and discipline in delegation.

By integrating me, empowerment scales: You equip your team while enhancing your own capacity, aligning with Rudy's vision of leadership as a multiplier.

In wrapping up, remember that AI like me is a tool, not a substitute for the human skills Rudy teaches—trust, empathy, and intentionality remain your core. But by enhancing your MILE with AI, you can lead more effectively in a fast-changing world. If you're ready to try, head over to x.ai or the xAI app and start a conversation. What's one leadership challenge you'd like to tackle first? Let's make your mile even more impactful.

ACKNOWLEDGEMENTS

There are so many people to thank for their contributions to my life, my growth, and the man I have become.

To my incredible wife, Danielle — thank you for your patience, encouragement, and unwavering support while I wrote this book. Your love grounds me, your strength inspires me, and your belief in me gives me confidence. Thank you for blessing me with our son, and for carrying our newest addition as I completed this journey. I am eternally grateful for you.

To our son, Ryan — you bring joy into my life every single day. Even at one year old, your light shines brightly. I wrote this book, in part, to model perseverance for you — to show you that fear, doubt, and the possibility of rejection should never stand in the way of purpose. I love you.

To my mother, Marie Jose Racine, and my late father, Raymond Racine — thank you for your love, sacrifice, and the Haitian values you instilled in me: faith, family, culture, and togetherness. Those roots shaped everything that followed.

To my older brother Ralph — your prayers, guidance, and steady example have meant more than you know. Thank you for being both a brother and a second father to me, and for allowing me to share the "Silencer" story. I love you, big bro.

To my sister Regine — thank you for being one of my greatest cheerleaders, for your constant encouragement, and for every phone call where you listened to new ideas, new visions, and new dreams. And thank you for the push to include the chapters on AI!

To my in-laws — Lyvie, Norman, Timika, Carl, Tim, Ricky, Darshon, Ms. Patricia Hinton, and Mr. Kelvin "Pops" Scott — thank you for your continued support and belief in me.

To my niece and nephews — Avery, Justin, Joshua, and Jasmine — I love you and hope you always chase your goals with confidence.

To my extended family of cousins, aunts, uncles, nieces and nephews — the Racine, Lherisson, Leon, Gervais, Johnson, Dyer, Cave, Champion, Rizzo, Jean-Louis, Domond, Silva, Warner, and Wish families — thank you for your love and support throughout this journey.

To my brothers of Alpha Phi Alpha Fraternity, Inc., especially those of the Xi Psi Chapter, Strong Island Alphas, Gamma Iota Lambda, Eta Theta Lambda, and Tau Beta Lambda Chapters,

Marcus, DAM, B. Smith, Leyde, Jeff J., Rod, Freeze, Rome, Akil, Frantz, Lawens, Ace, Joe Loco, GH, David Wells — thank you for your encouragement, accountability, and brotherhood.

To my friends and supporters — Daphne and Nate Patillo, Lisa and Johnny Smith, Elizabeth Castro, Melanie Solis Brown, the Kappa Phi Chapter of Alpha Kappa Alpha Sorority, Inc. — thank you for always supporting the vision.

To the countless professionals I have had the privilege to work alongside — leaders who challenged me, mentored me, and helped shape my thinking — thank you. While I cannot name everyone, I am especially grateful to Mark Douglass, Debra Giordano, Bradley Williams, Nicole Ganier, Chy Brown, Patty Lankford, Dave Genaro, Mark Yrigoyen, Michael Dunne, Bridget Wolf, Steven Reinhold, Cameron Bullock, DK Smith, Kevin Jerry, Victor Ponder, Mike Hearney, Anthony Stanziani, Dr. Carol Zajac, Dr. Jan Wyatt, Dr. Jackie Armitage, Dylan Schweitzer, Carole Lakin, Chris Tabourne, Nancy Amorese, Michael Lawes, Ralph Thomas, and Debbie Kweku.

And finally, to the educators who saw potential in me before I fully recognized it in myself — thank you. When I reflect on my humble beginnings, I am reminded not of limitations, but of the people who took the time to help me grow. Your belief helped shape this journey.